Media, Security and Sovereignty in the Canadian Arctic

This book documents how the Arctic region has been represented in the media: exploring how the media has framed the Arctic and whether this has an impact on governmental decision-making and public preferences.

The Arctic region faces profound transformations due to global warming, spurring intense debates about economic growth, environmental protection, and socio-cultural development. At the same time, most of humanity will never come face-to-face with the realities of the region: the media represents our only opportunity to learn about what this evolving region stands for. Recognizing that media coverage will tend to focus on specific events and relay specific messages, this book scrutinizes the nature of these messages to figure out how the Arctic region is presented by different media outlets. Studying different types of media, Landriault conducts an analysis of 628 newspaper articles, 110 televised reports, 9 magazine articles, and 404 tweets to provide the first systematic and rigorous study of Arctic media representations.

This book will interest scholars, practitioners, and students in Arctic studies, critical geography, political science, and communication studies.

Mathieu Landriault (PhD, 2013, University of Ottawa) is the director of the Observatoire de la Politique et la Sécurité de l'Arctique (OPSA), based in Montreal. He currently teaches at the School of Political Studies at the University of Ottawa as well as at the School of Conflict Studies at Saint Paul University. He is also an associate researcher at the Center for Interuniversity Research on the International Relations of Canada and Quebec (CIRRICQ). He is researching Arctic security, sovereignty, and governance issues in the circumpolar region in general and the Canadian Arctic in particular, as well as Arctic paradiplomacy.

Contents

Figures

Tables

Acknowledgements

This book is the result of three years of research and writing. I would first like to thank P. Whitney Lackenbauer, as his public call to provide more rigorous and systematic empirical evidence to support claims in Arctic scholarship represented a major source of inspiration to start this project.

I would also thank colleagues that have contributed their time or shared comments in order for this book to come to fruition: Frédéric Bastien, Rob Huebert, Franklyn Griffiths, P. Whitney Lackenbauer, Paul Minard, Elizabeth Elliot-Meisel, and Justin Massie.

Finally, I would like to thank my wife, Rachel, for her unconditional support, understanding and patience. Her insights and comments have been instrumental towards the completion of this book. This book would not have been possible without her.

Abbreviations

AEPS	Arctic Environmental Protection Strategy
AWPPA	Arctic Waters Pollution Prevention Act
CASS	Canadian Arctic security and sovereignty
CBC	Canadian Broadcasting Corporation
CF	Canadian Forces
DEW	Distant Early Warning
MP	Member of Parliament
NWP	Northwest Passage
PM	Prime Minister
PMO	Prime Minister's Office
RCMP	Royal Canadian Mounted Police
SDI	Strategic Defence Initiative
SOI	Students on Ice
UNCLOS	United Nations Convention on the Law of the Sea

Introduction

Media security, and sovereignty in the Canadian Arctic

The Arctic fascinates. Its remoteness and extreme environment have generated fear, speculation, and awe ever since European explorers first set foot in the region. The powerful symbols it generates abound: polar bears, remote communities, and once-thought perpetual ice are but a few examples. These strike the public's imagination and constitute good political resources for Canadian political elites. The Arctic's captivating aura also reaches the media where its symbolic resources can be tied to dominant narratives about global phenomenon. For example, a National Geographic video made public in December 2017 showed an emaciated polar bear struggling to survive. The caption opening the video was clear about the causal link inferred: "this is what climate change looks like." The magazine claimed that the video illustrated the consequences of climate change on the species, only to backtrack a few months later, stating that the publication did not tell the whole story and that "it was impossible to know why the bear was sick" (CBC, August 17 2018).

As to be expected, climate change significantly increased this fascination as the region entered a state of flux. Scholars in the social sciences have also been interested in the Arctic for many decades. In Canada, at the centre of this interest lies concerns about Canada's sovereignty. A heavy focus on international law could be discerned with scholars such as Donat Pharand, Donald McRae, Michael Byers, and Suzanne Lalonde producing high-quality scholarship from a legal perspective. On another front, authors such as Franklyn Griffiths, Rob Huebert and P. Whitney Lackenbauer focused on analyzing governmental policies while offering policy advice to Canadian decision-makers on how to best assert Canadian sovereignty over Canada's North.

This book wants to take a different path. International law or policy-advising focuses are crucial and productive; the scholars named above have offered incredible contributions to our understanding of

Arctic security and sovereignty. However, specific areas of inquiry have been ignored or marginalized as a result. For one, the media has not been studied seriously, as government and law dominated and still dominates the research agenda. This might come as a surprise, given that Arctic security and sovereignty is an "unobtrusive" issue, meaning an overwhelming majority of Canadians does not experience this issue in their day-to-day life (Soroka, 2002: p. 268). This characteristic usually makes the media more powerful since they can shape public perceptions about realities that everyday people cannot relate to on their own; the medium represents the sole provider of perceptions.

This book wants to fill this gap by empirically documenting when and how Arctic security and sovereignty issues have been portrayed in the Canadian media. The media sector is treated as an actor worth studying on its own terms focusing on the plurality and diversity of news outlets active in Canada. These media outlets are agents capable of influencing social and political actors in some instances while being influenced by these same actors in other instances. It becomes then crucial to understand the impact on and of political actors and institutions on media coverage. Hence, three questions will guide this research: (1) how were Arctic security and sovereignty issues portrayed in the Canadian media? (2) What type of media sources promoted specific types of meanings or understandings about these issues? (3) How media coverage influenced or was influenced by political actors?

These questions will be answered using a primarily inductive reasoning. Rather than assessing if grand theories materialized in media coverage, the emphasis will be put on gathering and assessing empirical evidence in order to understand how the Canadian media portrayed Arctic security and sovereignty issues. Such empirical observations can then act as a stepping stone to assess the nature of relationships and level of influence between the media, government, and public opinion.

To be honest, previous scholarship has brushed over the media's influence over Arctic issues in Canada. Let us look at how the media was studied (or not) in relation to the region in the two most significant crises over Arctic sovereignty, the 1969 Manhattan crisis and the 1985 Polar Sea crisis.

Crisis politics and the Canadian media

These two crises attracted attention and prompted government to act and implement measures. In the first instance, the company Humble Oil decided to send a tanker through the Northwest Passage (NWP) in August–September 1969 to test the feasibility of the route in order to transport newly discovered Alaskan oil to market. Months before the transit, "oil company executives and the U.S. Coast Guard consulted with Canadian officials and even requested that a Canadian icebreaker accompany the ship during its transit" (Coates et al., 2008: p. 95). Canada–US cooperation was high although the American government never asked for permission to go through the NWP, assuming it would negatively impact their claim that the waterway was an international strait rather than Canadian internal waters. This fact raised concerns in the Canadian population that Arctic sovereignty was challenged by their southern neighbour through the Manhattan's transit. The voyage went through as scheduled, escorted by Canadian and American icebreakers. The Government of Canada felt compelled to react to this crisis as public reactions were significant before, during, and after the crisis. As a result, the Trudeau government passed the Arctic Waters Pollution Prevention Act in April 1970, extending governmental reach through a non-discriminatory measure (pollution prevention rather than tariffs) within 100 nautical miles of Canadian Arctic coasts. Ultimately, Humble Oil decided to forego this route as the Manhattan had sustained significant damages (even with the escort of icebreakers) and costs and risks proved to be too high.

The second incident is eerily similar, this time starring a US Coast Guard icebreaker. In August 1985, the *Polar Sea* was partaking in a resupplying mission from an American military base in Greenland to Alaska, via the NWP. The American government supported the initiative as they claimed that the route was selected solely to save time and money, reassuring the Canadian government that the voyage was without prejudice for their sovereignty claims (Elliot-Meisel, 1999: p. 415). Again, the fact that the American government did not ask permission to their Canadian counterparts to go through the NWP provoked a public uproar, with many voices calling on the Canadian government to defend Arctic sovereignty more vigorously. Consequently, the federal government announced investments to step up Arctic capabilities while at the same time negotiating with the Americans to solve this matter once and for all (Howson, 1987–1988: pp. 341–4).

So in both cases, the Canadian public expressed concerns over what was perceived as a US challenge of Canadian Arctic sovereignty. The Government of Canada's approach in this second case was also strikingly similar to the first: exchanging with their American counterparts while holding a reassuring discourse to calm the public outrage. However, ultimately, the Canadian government reacted by implementing and/or announcing further measures to strengthen its Arctic sovereignty. In studying these two incidents, which role was attributed to the media by academics?

Seven of the most widely cited scholarly publications (six articles, one book chapter, and one book[1]) were analyzed in order to answer this question. Given the incredibly rich scholarship produced on these crises, our sample does not represent the totality of all analyses but it offers a glimpse of how the media was analyzed. Taken together, these eight publications have been widely cited[2].

Three observations can be extracted from how these texts studied the media. First, there is a surprising fusion between the Canadian media and public, in which the Canadian media and Canada's public opinion are not treated as distinct actors. Consequently, this makes it difficult to assess whether the media caused the public's reaction or if the influence went the other way around. For example, Elliot-Meisel (1999) wrote that:

> The United States informed Canada that it would also send a Coast Guard ship to assist the Manhattan. It did not ask for permission to enter the Passage, as that could be interpreted as recognition of Canadian sovereignty. Seen as a challenge to Canadian sovereignty claims by the Canadian public and media, calls for Canada to assert sovereignty prior to the transit increased.
>
> (p. 413)

She reiterated this media/public opinion fusion when referring to the Polar Sea crisis:

> the Canadian public and media did not believe the American claim that the sole purpose of utilizing the Passage was to save time. Reminiscent of the Manhattan voyage, they viewed the passage as "a direct threat to Canadian sovereignty."
>
> (p. 415)

Such perspective was also shared by Rothwell (1993) and McDorman (1986). Further, selected media commentators, columnists, and editorials were often used to illustrate Canadians reaction to specific events. For example, McDorman (1986) advanced that:

> great public concern was expressed in Canada that the passage of the Polar Sea was a violation of Canada's jurisdiction in the Arctic. The focus of media attention was that the United States did not and would not request from the Canadian Government permission for the Polar Sea to transit the Northwest Passage.
>
> (p. 625)

Howson (1987–1988) adopted the same approach. He presented Canadians' reaction to the Canadian government's reaction to the Polar Sea transit as "enthusiastic and congratulatory," using one columnist's piece (Jeffrey Simpson, *Globe and Mail*) as evidence.

Second, these authors shared a dominantly negative opinion of the media. The mildest critiques would point out minor factual mistakes committed by the Canadian media (McDorman, 1986: p. 624; Byers and Lalonde, 2009: p. 1174). However, others accused the Canadian press of propagating false information on these two events, popularizing misinterpretations about what actually transpired. The most incisive criticism came from Rothwell (1993) who presented the 1969 Manhattan incident as masterminded by the media:

> The controversy resulted primarily from the media created perception that the United States had refused to consult Canada over the voyage. Concern was also expressed over the potential maritime and environmental disaster which would occur if an oil tanker was involved in an accident while in Arctic waters. This anxiety, combined with the realization that Canada's legal position regarding the waters of the Northwest Passage and the Canadian Arctic was inconclusive, allowed the Manhattan's voyage through these waters to be portrayed as a direct threat to Canadian sovereignty which required an immediate Canadian response.
>
> (p. 337)

In Rothwell's analysis, the media was opportunistic in pursuing an ideological agenda, misrepresenting the American government's intention:

> The Canadian media took a strongly nationalistic view of the proposed voyage and, as had occurred in 1969 and 1970 with the Manhattan, saw the Polar Sea as a direct threat to Canadian sovereignty. This sentiment, combined with the apparent disregard by the United States for Canadian sensitivities, provided the media with an opportunity to condemn the voyage.
>
> (p. 343)

The press was also deemed cunning and mischievous in Coates et al.'s (2008) description of the *Manhattan* crisis. Here, the media ("the ways of the journalists") are depicted as opportunistically and ideologically exploiting the incident. In the authors' words, "The nationalist media jumped on this attitude (U.S. refusal to ask Canada's permission) as a direct affront to Canada's claims" (95–6).

Finally, the Canadian media were represented as highly influential, capable of generating crises and dictating the political agenda. This was expressed in the two previous citations from Rothwell, which state that the Canadian government has been compelled by the media to take a stronger stance vis-à-vis their American counterparts. This type of influence was also assumed to be effective after the 1988 Arctic agreement between both countries:

> Naval cooperation is both fiscally and politically "inexpensive," but the latter is true only if the issue of the Passage remains dormant. An "unauthorized" USN transit would undoubtedly inflame public opinion and media headlines, and resurrect a public relations and sovereignty nightmare for the government.
>
> (p. 422)

Coates et al. (2008) for their part put journalists in the "chattering class," alongside academics and civil society leaders, fusing the media with other social actors. These are said to have compelled the government to take action, masterminding the 1985 crisis: "The Canadian government's position soon began to shift as a result of vocal opposition" (114) from these forces. The government's response, thus, should be understood more as a reaction to popular pressure than to the voyage itself.

Now, to be fair, these three points may well be proven to be true. The media can at times, represent accurately what people think and may influence political representatives and force them to spend time on issues they would rather not address. The main problem here lies in the incompleteness of the empirical resources analyzed.

So how can this state of affair be explained? First, it should be pointed out that Arctic security and sovereignty experts used the media to raise awareness and publicly promote their respective points of view. As such, the media serves a purpose for these experts and this explains partially why experts have been, on the account of former Cabinet minister Bill Graham, "very effective in driving the Arctic sovereignty issue while he was in power" and "indirectly shaped political positions on the Arctic" (Chater, 2012: p. 834).

Second, the discipline in which they work carries part of the explanation. As many of the texts consulted were written from an international law perspective, we would not expect these contributions to spend a great deal of time and space documenting in details media reactions to these crises. However, some contributions (Elliot-Meisel, Coates et al. Huebert) did not undertake a legal study of these two

Media, Security and Sovereignty in the Canadian Arctic

From the Manhattan to the Crystal Serenity

Mathieu Landriault

LONDON AND NEW YORK

First published 2020
by Routledge
2 Park Square, Milton Park, Abingdon, Oxon OX14 4RN

and by Routledge
605 Third Avenue, New York, NY 10017

First issued in paperback 2021

Routledge is an imprint of the Taylor & Francis Group, an informa business

Publisher's Note
The publisher has gone to great lengths to ensure the quality of this reprint but points out that some imperfections in the original copies may be apparent.

British Library Cataloguing-in-Publication Data
A catalogue record for this book is available from the British Library

Library of Congress Cataloging-in-Publication Data
A catalog record has been requested for this book

ISBN 13: 978-1-03-224021-3 (pbk)
ISBN 13: 978-0-367-41806-9 (hbk)

Typeset in Times New Roman
by codeMantra

incidents. Coates *et al.*'s depiction of the role the media played in both crises is the most thoroughly researched contribution. However, the breadth of resources and sources consulted in it is not comprehensive and is rather selective. Further, many questions remain unanswered: did we see different coverage across different types of media (TV, radio, newspapers)? Can we observe similar framing in editorials and journalistic articles? Were there alternative framings disseminated in the media? Did the media influence public opinion and civil society or did the press merely react to civil society's protest? Did media activism influence durably public opinion preferences months or years after these crises?

This perspective on the media also raises an interesting question: if the media were so influential and critical in the advent of these two crises, why is it that no study systematically measured and focused on its role? More troubling is the quasi-absence of such focus after the *Polar Sea* crisis…

Out of crisis mode – Canadian media after the Polar Sea

The 1990s represented a quieter period in regards to Canadian Arctic security and sovereignty matters. Far from crises and anxieties, the region was treated as an ideal venue to reap the peace dividend of the post-Cold War, mostly by developing regional governance institutions and fostering cooperative endeavours. The Arctic Environmental Protection Strategy (AEPS), launched in 1991, turned into a more institutionalized form of cooperation when the Arctic Council was officially created in 1996. The Canadian government has been instrumental in making this process fruitful and fostering environmental cooperation between the eight Arctic states (Scrivener, 1999).

The Northern Dimension of Canada's Foreign Policy, published in 2000 by Canada's Department of Foreign Affairs and International Trade, encapsulates the approach of that decade. The document was concerned with environmental issues, imbued by a human security focusing on cooperation across borders and fostering sustainable development, trade opportunities for Northern people and educative opportunities (Department of Foreign Affairs and International Trade, 2000).

On the defence side of the equation, for experts like Rob Huebert, "it is clear that the Arctic simply ceased being an area of significant concern for Canadian security during the 1990s" (Huebert, 2006: p. 22). Important cuts to surveillance done by the Canadian Forces in the region pointed in the direction of a decrease of activism on the defence of sovereignty aspect. No substantial controversy or Polar

Sea-like crisis emerged during this time period, as a bilateral agreement with the American partner reduced the likelihood of a repeated sovereignty crisis. Lack of sustained interest or attention in the region could explain, to a certain extent, why no time was devoted studying Canadian media representations of the Arctic; a calm sea is typically no news and while silences could be more telling than words, they are typically not the subject of great academic scholarship.

However, the lack of attention on the media in the years that were to follow is more disconcerting. Indeed, the 2000s saw the emergence of climate change and more specifically global warming as phenomenon that had the potential of radically changing geographic and material realities in the circumpolar region. The most fundamental element of this environment, a permanent or semi-permanent ice cover, was and still is under threat, creating uncertainty as to the impact that ice disappearance or reduction would have on geopolitical relations. Debates focused on determining the extent of these changes (more on this in Chapter 2), but one fact remained: change would occur. This prompted many analysts to offer security and sovereignty assessments, predicting how the political and economic Arctic environment would evolve as a result of thinning ice. The region was entering a state of flux and different actors (media, experts, governments) were reframing the region in new terms, using new (or in some cases, recycled) language and images.

At the very least, global warming and its consequences on the Arctic attracted a great amount of media coverage. As Coates et al. (2008) put it,

> suddenly, after decades of being coffee-table conversation for academics, the Canadian Arctic is front-page news – in the *New York Times*, in *Time* magazine and in papers around the world – and because of the melting ice cap that according to Al Gore threatens to drown the coastlines of the world, has a prominent place in his documentary, *An Inconvenient Truth*.
>
> (p. 137)

The Canadian media was also vocal participants in the sovereignty crises that punctuated the decade, from Hans island (summer 2005) to the USS Charlotte incident (Winter 2005) and the drop of the Russian flag at the bottom of the Arctic Ocean (summer 2007) (Landriault, 2013).

All in all, the period was characterized by great activism, the media being a non-negligible actor in this effort. Surprisingly, scholarly attention on the media was scarce. There were a few exceptions, but too often, analyzing media coverage was anecdotal and reminiscent of the analytical focus deployed to scrutinize media influence during the 1969 and 1985 crises: non-comprehensive and quite selective. Elizabeth Riddell-Dixon (2008), for example, set out to debunk assumptions about the Arctic continental shelf that had been spread out publicly by the media. Selective media headlines and stories were presented in this work to document the true nature of the process around the delimitation of the continental shelf. As such, this did little to inform us on whether this catastrophe scenario angle was widespread in the media or limited to specific outlets or even if the catchy nature of the headlines betrayed the nature of the subsequent text, more reassuring and balanced. Of course, again, this contribution does not have the media as main focus; international law remains the primary focal point of the analysis.

Lackenbauer also referred to the media while describing the policy environment on Arctic issues in Canada. This context is characterized by counter-productive fear-mongering:

> "if muckraking academics and journalists are to be believed, the circumpolar agenda is now dominated by a 'polar race' with a concomitant sovereignty and security crisis precipitated by climate change and competing interests in 'our' Arctic" [...] In the early twenty-first century, amidst rhetoric about a "new Cold War" in the Arctic, commentators suggest that cooperative arrangements are less credible. In a supposed "race for resources," the Russians, Americans, Danes and other energy-hungry nations are alleged to threaten Canada's northern inheritance.
>
> (2011: p. 70)

A similar undertaking was done by Franklyn Griffiths, who perceived media agents as purveyors of polar peril. For Griffiths (2011),

> Promoted by academic purveyors of polar peril and amplified by the media an unwarranted sense of Arctic vulnerability has come upon us. Prone to exaggerated threat assessment and overly insistent on the need for hardware to assert control, Canadians in the grip of possession anxiety are given to self-doubt when actually the outlook is good [...] Canadians worry, and journalists and editorialists feed on this worry. Sensationalism becomes the order of the day in commentary on a part of the world very few know much about.
>
> (p. 213)

These assertions, however, are presented as a given and not proven empirically or documented systematically; they require comprehensive empirical testing to measure their relative prevalence compared to other types of assessments and their temporal dissemination.

When looking at the Arctic region as a whole, a push to focus on media perceptions of the Arctic can be observed in recent years. Russian media has been under the microscope, with findings that the media sector closely followed governmental policies (Wilson-Rowe, 2013; Gritsenko, 2016). A comprehensive study was undertaken by Steinberg et al. (2014), systematically documenting and analyzing media perceptions and framing of Arctic issues in press organizations from 20 countries. Their work focused on a high number of countries. However, they sampled on a limited temporal focus and reviewed only a limited number of actual articles (280). The limited timeline represents the main handicap as media perceptions of the 2013 Kiruna Arctic Council meeting is the sole focal point, restricting analysis on the evolution of these perceptions as well as establishing if these representations mark a turning point in traditional or historical media frames on Arctic issues in these publications. Highly salient events offer an interesting entry point into analyzing how the media covers the Arctic since media attention is greater during these climatic moments; however, it begs the question if these events represent dominant perceptions of Arctic issues. We do not know, for example, if these perceptions were durable and if they persisted after these brief episodes, if they stuck to public consciousness or media practices. Likewise, the empirical demonstration in Pincus and Ali (2016) was not rigorous and consistent, focusing rather on how agenda setting and framing could be applied to media coverage of the Arctic.

The literature about the Canadian media's take on the Arctic is also in its infancy stage. Nicol's (2013) study of media depictions of the Canadian Arctic was one of the first contributions focusing on the Canadian media and the Arctic. Looking at major daily Canadian newspapers, she studied their journalistic article content in the 1970s as well as in 1989, 1999, 2009, and 2013. Her study concluded that media discourses are dominated by state-centric views and deals with four themes (resource development, science and environment, military and security issues, and cultural life/practices; Nicol, 2013: pp. 3–4). While representing a worthwhile and salutary contribution, the extended time period did not allow to go in-depth on specific time periods. Media analyses on Arctic issues in Canada remain at an embryonic stage, especially considering the relatively low volume of empirical data gathered and analyzed. For example, others have contributed elsewhere at putting the media on the spotlight by looking at specific media resources (editorials, e.g., see Landriault, 2013) or specific topic (on the Arctic Council, see Chater and Landriault, 2016; on climate change, see Stoddart and Smith, 2016; on the Rangers, see Lackenbauer, 2018). These efforts are still isolated and general observations are difficult to generate at this point in time.

Much work needs to be done dissecting media perceptions of the Canadian Arctic in order to gain thorough understanding of their role and influence in shaping Arctic security and sovereignty issues. Studying the media has the potential of furthering our understanding of what Canadian Arctic security and sovereignty actually means.

Media as discourses of security and sovereignty

What can we learn about Arctic security and sovereignty from analyzing the media? The question is relevant since we could consider the media as epiphenomenal, a secondary phenomenon merely a reaction or response to something else (be it government or public opinion, for example). However, focusing on the media permits us to unpack the meaning of security and sovereignty by looking at competing discourses promoting different interpretations of what is meant by security and sovereignty. It points towards the constructed nature of security and sovereignty assessments. In terms of security, for example, the question of who should be secured and why are inherent to the idea of security; from this standpoint, "winning the right to define security provides not just access to resources but also the authority to articulate new definitions and discourses of security" (Lipschutz, 1995: p. 8). To talk about security issues and spread diagnostics as to the levels of danger created by different threats is to shape security in one way or another. As Simon Dalby (2002) pointed out,

> Security is about the future or fears about the future. It is about contemporary dangers but also thwarting potential future dangers. It is about control, certainty, and predictability in an uncertain world [...] Security provides narratives of danger as the stimulus to collective action.
>
> (p. 163)

Hence, security is a contested concept, generating different interpretations as to what the future might look like and how to tackle current and emerging threats. The fact that we have lively debates as to what are Arctic security threats and how to address them testifies to the dynamic nature of the concept. A similar observation can be made for sovereignty, especially in the Canadian Arctic; proposed strategies or roadmaps to assert or bolster Canadian Arctic sovereignty claims vary depending on the analyst consulted. Inuit conceptions of security and sovereignty are a case in point proving this diversity of point of views (e.g., see Inuit Tapiriit Kanatami, 2013).

As such, the media can be understood as an actor spreading certain understandings and assessments on Canadian Arctic security and sovereignty. The media is a valuable subject of interest for scholarly inquiry since it allows us to assess which of these understandings are dominant, when they are and to which rationale or justification they are tied to.

However, it appears important at this stage to situate the media vis-à-vis other political actors. This book is not of the opinion that the media single-handedly force governments into action or impose ideas about people. The propaganda theory of the media assumes a rather simplistic causal relationship, downplaying the freedom and leeway exercised by the audience or government in their dealings with the media and media stories. The media is a fascinating actor to research, precisely because of its complex nature and the variable degrees of influence on government and people it has. Many temporal and contextual variables can come in to play, making one issue or story salient at one point in time but not at another. Blanket assumptions on their role are, therefore, blinding our view on their actual social and political role. The media can also be influenced by cultural norms and governmental policies; news outlets do not exist in a void. They often react to governmental messaging and are catering to an audience. As such, they are not perfectly free to diffuse specific messages.

Thus, we conceptualize the media as part of a broader public policy environment. As a societal actor, they influence "the bounds within which the government has to operate" by promoting what they consider to be acceptable options and focusing on priorities and decisions that they deem important (Nossal et al., 2015: p. 119). The media reports on actors, events, and issues, informing the Canadian population at the same time as influencing them by focusing on some events and not others and situating these events in broader narratives.

The media can act on the policy environment in three different ways. First, it can partake in agenda setting by "making some issues more salient in people's mind" (Scheufele and Tewksbury, 2007: p. 11). As such, the media can dictate the political agenda as "the public learns the relative importance of issues from the amount of coverage given to the issues in the news media" (Wanta et al., 2004: p. 367). This can also influence governmental decision-makers. As Savoie (1999) observed,

> reading the memoirs of former federal Cabinet ministers or listening to interviews with them reflecting on their years in office, one is struck by the number of references to what they consider relatively minor issues which came to receive a great deal of media attention and to dominate the government agenda, if only for brief periods of time.
>
> (p. 314)

Such influence does not work in all circumstances. The nature of the issue (Soroka, 2002), the amount of consensus among political actors, and past popular understandings on an issue (Scheufele and Tewksbury, 2007: pp. 12–17) are factors which explain why agenda setting works on some issues or in some contexts and not in others.

Second, political messaging of key Arctic actors constitutes an interesting area of research. Here, political messaging refers to how political actors, for example, government, publicly promote and explain their decisions and actions. The media is often harnessed to achieve these objectives. Hence, studying political messaging entails analyzing how political actors used the media to further their interests.

Finally, media framing is about how events and issues are portrayed and explained in the news media. An issue frame is, therefore, "a theme, story line, or label suggesting a preferred interpretation of some policy question" (Richardson and Lancendorf, 2005: p. 75). These interpretive cues (Vucetic, 2016: p. 235) are thought to have an influence on how the issue is understood and perceived by the audience (Scheufele and Tewksbury, 2007: p. 11). This technique can be found in editorials and in journalistic reports. Framing highlights the different interpretations that one can make while giving meaning to Arctic issues and events. The signification, the aspects of the story emphasized on or the nature of the issue at hand are all tools that the media and journalists can use to perform framing, whether intentionally or not. Framing and agenda setting fuse when one evaluates which framing is the most widespread one among many available issue frames. As prominent Arctic expert Rob Huebert argued when interviewed for this book, the media can have an effect on government decision albeit a reinforcing one; repetition of the same statement can reach decision-makers, especially if it supports what they want to hear. Hence, repetition of an issue frame can move political actors.

Agenda setting, political messaging, and framing prove to be three useful tools when evaluating the media's influence on government and society. They are also versatile enough to allow us to consider how political and social actors (government, civil society groups, experts) use the media and influence the messages spread by them. Moreover, these techniques can be found in different types of media (social media, television, radio, and newspapers) and can help answer two key questions: what is covered when one talks about the Arctic in the media and how is it covered?

The way forward

This book is the first systematic, empirically grounded attempt at exploring how the Canadian media represents Arctic security and sovereignty issues.

This book will be divided as follows. Chapter 1 will focus on providing the first detailed empirical evidence of media coverage during the 1969 Manhattan and the 1985 Polar Sea crises. Agenda setting and framing will be scrutinized to document the role played by the press during these two crises.

Chapter 2 will be concerned with analyzing dominant framing present in journalistic articles published in Canadian newspapers from June 2000 to April 2005. This time period coincides with the publication of two important, albeit quite different, policy documents issued by the Government of Canada. The chapter will assess the role played by experts in framing the region during this crucial period.

Chapter 3 will detail media representations of the Prime Minister's annual Arctic tour, from 2006 to 2014. These tours, held every August by then Prime Minister Stephen Harper, acted as attention-grabbing events, highlighting the importance of the region. Television news broadcasts will attract our attention, and media reactions to the government's political messaging will be scrutinized to assess its diffusion.

In Chapter 4, the links between media and public opinion will be put under the microscope. The 2010–2015 period will be our focus of interest since those were the years in which the most comprehensive inquiries on public preferences on Arctic issues, the 2010 and 2015 Rethinking the Top of the World polls, were conducted. Chapter 4 will detail the media environment at play during this time period; newspapers and television news broadcasts will be the empirical resources used to describe what types of message about the Arctic reached the Canadian people. Agenda setting will be at the centre of the analysis on this extended period of time, focusing on Arctic Council meetings.

Finally, Chapter 5 will focus on social media to assess whether they change the nature of the discussion on Arctic security and sovereignty issues. Twitter will serve as empirical evidence to uncover Arctic representations present in new media. A case study will occupy our attention. The voyage of the cruise ship Crystal Serenity, during the summer of 2016, will offer us a glimpse into social media's role in framing the Canadian Arctic. This will also allow this book to compare traditional and social media coverage of the very same event.

Notes

1 These publications are: McDorman (1986), In the Wake of the "Polar Sea", Howson (1987–1988), Breaking the Ice, Rothwell (1993), The Canadian-U.S. Northwest Passage Dispute; Elliot-Meisel (1999), Still Unresolved after Fifty Years, Pharand (2007), The Arctic Waters and the Northwest Passage, Coates et al. (2008), Arctic Front, Byers and Lalonde (2009), Who Controls the Northwest Passage?, Huebert (2011), Climate Change and Canadian Sovereignty.

2 Cited 526 times to be more precise, according to the search engine Google Scholar.

References

Byers, Michael and Lalonde, Suzanne. 2009. Who Controls the Northwest Passage. *Vanderbilt Journal of Transnational Law*, volume 42: pp. 1133–210.

CBC. August 17 2018. National Geographic Says It "Went Too Far" with Emaciated Polar Bear Video. *CBC News*, available at www.cbc.ca/news/canada/north/emaciated-polar-bear-response-1.4788259

Chater, Andrew. 2012. Beyond the "Golly-Gee" Stage. *International Journal*, volume 67, issue 3: pp. 831–47.

Chater, Andrew and Landriault, Mathieu. 2016. Understanding Media Perceptions of the Arctic Council. *Arctic Yearbook*, volume 5: pp. 60–72.

Coates, Ken, Lackenbauer, P. Whitney, Morrison, William and Poelzer, Greg. 2008. *Arctic Front – Defending Canada in the Far North*. Thomas Allen Publishers, Toronto.

Dalby, Simon. 2002. *Environmental Security*. University of Minnesota Press, Minnesota.

Department of Foreign Affairs and International Trade of Canada. 2000. The Northern Dimension of Canada's Foreign Policy (last checked August 31 2016) http://gac.canadiana.ca/view/ooe.b3651149E/1?r=0&s=1

Elliot-Meisel, Elisabeth. 1999. Still Unresolved after Fifty Years: The Northwest Passage in Canadian-American Relations, 1946–1998. *The American Review of Canadian Studies*, volume 29, issue 3: pp. 407–30.

Griffiths, Franklyn. 2011. Towards a Canadian Arctic Strategy. In Franklyn Griffiths, Rob Huebert, and P. Whitney Lackenbauer (eds.) *Canada and the Changing Arctic*. Wilfrid Laurier University Press, Waterloo: pp. 181–215.

Gritsenko, Daria. 2016. Vodka on Ice? Unveiling Russian Media Perceptions of the Arctic. *Energy Research and Social Science*, volume 16: pp. 8–12.

Howson, Nicholas. 1987–1988. Breaking the Ice: The Canadian-American Dispute over the Arctic 's Northwest Passage. *Columbia Journal of Transnational Law*, volume 26: pp. 337–76.

Huebert, Rob. 2006. Renaissance in Canadian Arctic Security? *Canadian Military Journal,* volume 6, winter: pp. 17–29.

Huebert, Rob. 2011. Climate Change and Canadian Sovereignty in the Northwest Passage. In P. Whitney Lackenbauer (ed.) *Canadian Arctic Sovereignty and Security: Historical Perspectives*, Calgary Papers in Military and Strategic Studies, Occasional Paper number 4: pp. 383–99.

Inuit Tapiriit Kanatami. 2013. Nilliajut: Inuit Perspectives on Security, Patriotism and Sovereignty. Munk-Gordon Arctic Security Program, Working Papers on Arctic Security Series, available at www.gordonfoundation.ca/publication/626

Lackenbauer, P. Whitney. 2011. From Polar Race to Polar Saga – An Integrated Strategy for Canada and the Circumpolar World. In Franklyn Griffiths, Rob Huebert, and P. Whitney Lackenbauer (eds.) *Canada and the Changing Arctic*. Wilfrid Laurier University Press, Waterloo: pp. 69–179.

Lackenbauer, P. Whitney. 2018. "Indigenous Communities Are at the Heart of Canada's North": Media Misperceptions of the Canadian Rangers, Indigenous Services, and Arctic Security. *Journal of Military and Strategic Studies*, volume 19, issue 2: pp. 157–92.

Landriault, Mathieu. 2013. La sécurité arctique 2000–2010: une décennie turbulente? Ph.D. Dissertation, University of Ottawa, available at www.ruor.uottawa.ca/handle/10393/24353

Lipschutz, Ronnie. 1995. On Security. In Ronnie Lipschutz (ed.) *On Security*. Columbia University Press, New York: pp. 1–23.

McDorman, Ted. 1986. In the Wake of the "Polar Sea": Canadian Jurisdiction and the Northwest Passage. *Les cahiers de droit*, volume 27, issue 3: pp. 623–46.

Nicol, Heather. 2013. Natural News, State Discourses and The Canadian Arctic. *Arctic Yearbook*.

Nossal, Kim Richard, Roussel, Stéphane and Paquin, Stéphane. 2015. *The Politics of Canadian Foreign Policy*. McGill-Queen's University Press, Montréal.

Pharand, Donald. 2007. The Arctic Waters and the Northwest Passage: A Final Revisit. *Ocean Development and International Law*, volume 38: pp. 3–69.

Pincus, Rebecca and Ali, Saleem. 2016. Have You Been to "The Arctic"? Frame Theory and the Role of Media Coverage in Shaping Arctic Discourse. *Polar Geography*, volume 39, issue 2: pp. 83–97.

Richardson, John and Lancendorf, Karen. 2004. Framing Affirmative Action – The Influence of Race on Newspaper Editorial Responses to the University of Michigan Cases. *The International Journal of Press/Politics*, volume 9: pp. 74–94.

Riddell-Dixon, Elizabeth. 2008. Canada and Arctic Politics: The Continental Shelf Extension. *Ocean Development and International Law*, volume 39, issue 4: pp. 343–59.

Rothwell, Donald. 1993. The Canadian-U.S. Northwest Passage Dispute: A Reassessment. *Cornell International Law Journal*, volume 26: pp. 331–72.

Savoie, Donald. 1999. Governing from the Centre. University of Toronto Press, Toronto.

Scheufele, Dietram and Tewksbury, David. 2007. Framing, Agenda Setting, and Priming: The Evolution of Three Media Effects Models. *Journal of Communication*, volume 57: pp. 9–20.

Scrivener, David. 1999. Arctic Environmental Cooperation in Transition. *Polar Record*, volume 35, issue 192: pp. 51–8.

Soroka, Stuart. 2002. Issue Attributes and Agenda-Setting by Media, the Public, and Policymakers in Canada. *International Journal of Public Opinion Research*, volume 14, issue 3: pp. 264–85.

Steinberg, Philip, Bruun, Johanne and Medby, Ingrid. 2014. Covering Kiruna: A Natural Experiment in Arctic Awareness. *Polar Geography*, volume 37: pp. 273–97.

Stoddard, Mark and Smith, Jillian. 2016. The Endangered Arctic, the Arctic as Resource Frontier: Canadian News Media Narratives of Climate Change and the North. *Canadian Review of Sociology*, volume 53, issue 3: pp. 316–36.

Vucetic, Srdjan. 2016. Who Framed the F-35? Government-media Relations in Canadian Defence Procurement. *International Journal*, volume 71, issue 2: pp. 231–48.

Wanta, Wayne, Golan, Guy and Lee, Cheolhan. 2004. Agenda Setting and International News: Media Influence on Public Perceptions of Foreign Nations. *Journalism and Mass Communication Quarterly*, volume 81, issue 2: pp. 364–77.

Wilson-Rowe, Elana. 2013. A Dangerous Space? Unpacking State and Media Discourses on the Arctic. *Polar Geography*, volume 36: pp. 232–44.

1 The Canadian media and Arctic sovereignty crises

As specified in the introduction, scholars focusing on Arctic sovereignty blamed the media for past sovereignty crises. Indeed, it is widely accepted that the media had an agenda-setting effect, by devoting attention to the region and compelling national decision-makers to react more forcefully than originally planned. However, how this agenda-setting outcome came to materialize was not sufficiently documented by these same experts. This chapter has the ambition of providing the first systematic study of how the Canadian media successfully attracted public interest to these events.

Agenda setting has been investigated in numerous studies, for the most part tackling the phenomenon in two different ways. First-level agenda setting has focused on object salience, typically measuring the amount of coverage given by the media to a topic or event where more coverage equals more importance. However, second-level agenda setting set out to define agenda setting by also analyzing issue frames present in the media. The idea is that the manner in which these items are described will also have an impact on issue salience (Wanta et al., 2004: pp. 366–9). This chapter will investigate both first and second-level agenda settings to analyze media treatment of the 1969 Manhattan and 1985 Polar Sea crises.

The Canadian media and the 1969 Manhattan crisis

The 1969 Manhattan crisis did not constitute the only episode of controversies regarding Canada's Northern sovereignty: discussions on the establishment of the Distant Early Warning System with the United States in the late 1950s also created tensions and debates in Canadian society and government. However, this crisis represented the most acute episode on Canada's Arctic sovereignty at that time – one that did not lead to easy or immediate solutions. The timeline studied begins with the first instances of media attention in mid-May 1969, and end soon after the return trip of the second Manhattan expedition in late June 1970. The *Globe and Mail* coverage was analyzed, using the keyword "Manhattan."[1] In total, 170 news articles and editorials were published, with 62% of them having the Manhattan as their primary focus of interest.[2]

As may be observed in Figure 1.1, media attention peaked twice during the time period under scrutiny: once in September 1969 and a second time in March 1970. Articles for which the Manhattan was the primary focus also peaked at the same time.

Rather than garnering attention, media coverage followed a cycle of wave, receding from October 1969 to January 1970, before picking up steam from February to April only to decline in May and June 1970. Focusing on a more specific timeline, the initial response by government did not seem to have been spurred by overwhelming media attention. At first,

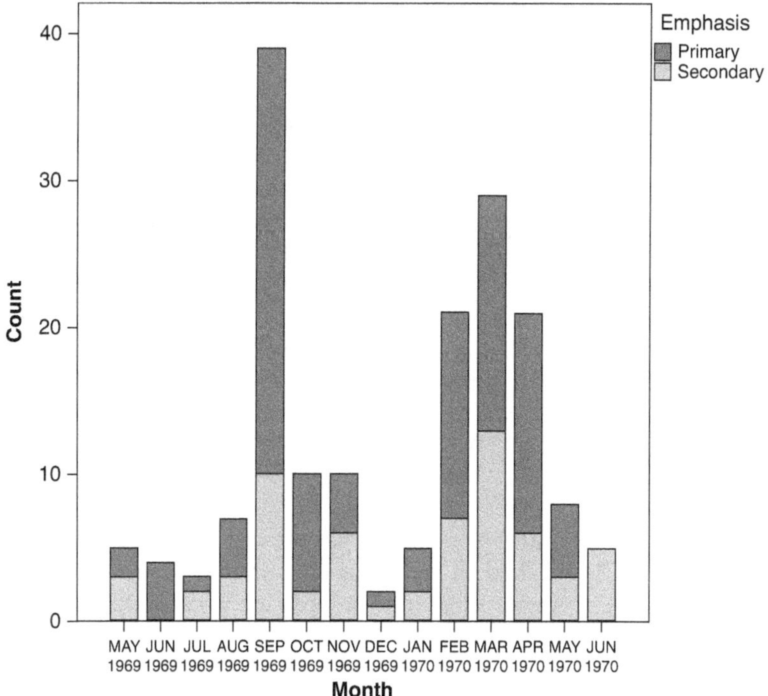

Figure 1.1 Number of newspaper articles published in the *Globe and Mail* with the term "Manhattan" by level of interest.

Note: All graphs in this book have been generated using SPSS.

Prime Minister Pierre Elliot Trudeau and key ministers offered reassuring answers, downplaying the seriousness of the situation. Trudeau told Canadians that "the legal status of the waters of Canada's Arctic archipelago is not at issue with the proposed voyage," adding, however, that "it is also known that not all countries would accept the view that the waters between the islands and the archipelago are internal waters over which Canada has full sovereignty" (*Globe and Mail*, June 28 1969: p. 11). The Manhattan was mostly framed as an economic opportunity before the transit by the Prime Minister while he visited Churchill:

> Canada had to make a choice – leave some things underdeveloped or undeveloped, or to have them done with the aid of foreign capital [...] Mr. Trudeau said he could see nothing wrong with the ship of a friendly nation testing the feasibility of transporting oil from the region.
>
> (*Globe and Mail*, July 15 1969: p. 4)

In fact, only a few articles were written before a change of policy and tone could be noticed from government. Indeed, External Affairs Minister Mitchell Sharp announced on 2 September 1969 that "a definitive statement on Canada's claims to sovereignty in Arctic waters will be made some time within the next few months" (*Globe and Mail*, September 3 1969: p. B1), a statement that, while being relatively vague, acted as a reaction to perceived popular pushback. In all, only 21 articles were published before 2 September 1969, even if unexpected developments could have caused greater media exposure. For one, two barges, the *John A. Norburg* and the *Learmonth*, operated by Panarctic (a joint venture between Canadian companies and the federal government) were punctured by ice on 21 August and ultimately sank near Melville Island. The Norburg represented a potential environmental hazard, containing thousands of gallons of diesel fuel (Watkins, August 28 1969: p. B2). The accident highlighted the perils of Arctic navigation, particularly when dealing with oil transportation.

It would not be until 5 September that the first *Globe and Mail* editorial was to be published, more than a week after the departure of the Manhattan on 25 August. The editorial was short on solutions, rather criticizing the "negligent" governmental handling of the transit and calling it a nasty precedent for Canadian Arctic sovereignty. However, Sharp's announcement was welcomed with cautious hope: "all we can hope for at present is Mr. Sharp's statement, after Mr. Sharp has been told, in a meeting this fall, what the United States will accept" (*Globe and Mail*, September 5 1969: p. 6).

Sharp's announcement did not mean that the Manhattan was no longer on the media's radar. In fact, most media reports peaked in September, after the 2 September announcement. Two types of stories dominated media coverage between 2 September and 24 October, at which time the Prime Minister delivered a speech indicating that government would impose pollution control regulations in its Arctic waters.

First, the very nature of the Manhattan transit generated the most media coverage. The most popular framing of the issue served to assess whether the transit was a success or a failure, emphasizing on the fact that the voyage was a precedent. In the *Globe and Mail*, such framing resulted in detailing the obstacles that the Manhattan had encountered all the while, informing readers on how the Canadian icebreaker (the *John, A. Macdonald*) assisted the American vessel. In total, 14 news articles described the Manhattan transit and the functions performed by the John A. Macdonald. The presence of American journalists (and the Canadian Press) aboard the Manhattan and Canadian journalists aboard the John A. Macdonald helped insure significant, almost day-to-day coverage of the expedition.

A second type of story often covered in the *Globe and Mail* focused on governmental responsiveness to the transit. Past the initial passive stance, Cabinet became proactive at defusing the tension produced by its initial response. Nine (9) news articles had for main purpose to report or react to a minister's public address on the upcoming Arctic statement. For the most part, External Affairs minister Mitchell Sharp was the main protagonist, reinsuring Canadians that a new legislation tackling maritime pollution in the Arctic would be introduced soon, with the *Globe and Mail* offering Sharp a full page to explain the government's point of view. Prime Minister Trudeau, National Defence Minister Léo Cadieux and Northern Development Minister Jean Chrétien carried the same message when delivering talks at other venues.

This strategy paid off as the announcement of a future Arctic statement calmed the clamour. In a subsequent editorial on 13 September, the *Globe and Mail* deemed the idea of the statement reasonable. The editorial then turned to necessary investments in order to ensure control over the region, describing Arctic waters as vital to Canadian well-being (*Globe and Mail*, September 13 1969: p. 6). A later editorial also made clear that the initial governmental strategy to deny that the Manhattan raised sovereignty issues was ill-advised, even for a rather centrist and moderate newspaper like the *Globe and Mail*.[3] According to the newspaper, "Canadians could be forgiven for suspecting that the Government is sitting on the issue's head in the hopes that it will not arise," further pointing to the Canadian government's passive approach towards Arctic sovereignty since the early 1960s (*Globe and Mail*, September 19 1969). It would, therefore, seem obvious that the statement on pollution control in Arctic waters acted as an acceptable solution to address the crisis.

The quasi absence of organized civil society opposition somewhat limited media coverage. The most vocal opposition came from within the governing party's rank. Members of the House of Commons Northern Development and Indian Affairs committee flew to the Arctic in order to conduct what they called an "inspection tour" of the tanker (*Globe and Mail*, August 29 1969: p. 25). The group members, led by Liberal MPs, were quite critical of the governmental position, voicing environmental protection and citing the loss of the two Panarctic barges as signs of risks for upcoming oil transportation. Furthermore, they were vocal on sovereignty issues, rebutting arguments that the status of Arctic waterways was up for debate. However, this opposition was only able to capture minimal media attention.

The Arctic pollution protection legislation was only introduced in late October. The vagueness of the upcoming bill contributed to the second media coverage peak, this time over a longer timeline (February–April). Media attention was more significant ahead of the second transit. Between the public announcement of the second transit (2 February 1970) and its actual departure (3 April 1970), 50 news articles mentioned the Manhattan. It is fair to say that political parties played an important role in making the issue salient. As the event happened before deliberations in the House of Commons were broadcasted, the *Globe and Mail* offered a transcript of Question Period to its readership. The issue was raised no less than nine times by Opposition MPs over a two-month period.

Opposition parties were quite skilful at zeroing in on the proposed bills' shortcomings. A minority of their interventions were centred on the necessity for the government to issue a "unilateral claim to Canadian jurisdiction over all the waters of the Arctic archipelago" (Newman, February 14 1970: p. 4). The confusing political messaging of the acting government did not help to dissipate the controversy. On 19 February 1970, External Affairs Minister Mitchell Sharp displayed a contrastingly assertive attitude towards the dispute:

> These are our waters. There has never been any question of that. We have always regarded them as our waters. The question may be whether other people regard them as our waters – but that is

> another matter [...] It would be difficult to argue that the Arctic waters between Canadian territory have been regarded as part of the high seas.
>
> (Sharp cited in Newman, February 20 1969: p. 1)

The timing for these comments is intriguing: they were made one day after the publication of the most critical Globe editorial. Published on 18 February, the opinion piece called the government's approach towards Arctic sovereignty pusillanimous, meek and riddled with pious platitudes. It further enunciated a list of conditions to meet before any new transit:

> We should not let them come until the rules that will govern their presence have been settled; until the research into their potential for trouble has been completed; until the safeguards that should be taken have been determined and agreed upon; and until the challenge to our ultimate authority and responsibility in the archipelago has been faced and resolved.
>
> (*Globe and Mail*, February 18 1970: p. 6)

The text embodied a nationalist turn taken by the nation's most influential newspaper. As a result, Sharp's comments were worthy of front page attention, displaying assertiveness and authority. Nonetheless, this meant a sharp departure from a previous position and, as a result, put the Prime Minister on the defensive, with the PM electing to either dodge questions on his ministers' comments or making strange comments raising further questions[4] (*Globe and Mail*, February 25 1970: p. B2). Past Sharp's outburst, government was content with delaying any statement or answering questions in a meaningful way until the pollution control bill be put up for debate in the House of Commons in early April.

However, the announcement of a possible second Manhattan transit in early February forced the government to detail its approach. It seemed that the devil was in the details for Opposition MPs, resulting in significant media coverage. First, questions in late February were raised on the possibility that the Canadian government might deny the Manhattan transit if it was found that the tanker may not withstand ice pressure.

Subsequently, the need for an inspection of the said tanker was put front and centre: an inspection of the vessel was set as a prerequisite before granting icebreaker assistance, a condition that was not put in place for the first transit. The inspection had for primary focus to test if the Manhattan could meet Arctic shipping and pollution regulations that would be part of the upcoming bill. Issues such as whether the company, Humble Oil, agreed or not to regulations, the amount of the bond imposed on the company in case of oil spill, the calendar for the inspection process as well as the results of the inspection ensured that the second Manhattan transit was on the media radar. In fact, close to 60% of articles mentioning the Manhattan between 3 March (the day the inspection was announced) and 3 April (the day the Manhattan departed) had for primary focus the inspection process and the regulations imposed on the tanker.

Past the precedent of the first transit, media attention focused more heavily on the legislative and regulatory processes than on the transit itself. The Globe did not delegate any of its reporters to go aboard the ship to cover the transit, relying instead on the Canadian Press to do so. Media attention shifted after the introduction of the Arctic Waters Pollution Prevention bill in early June. Afterwards, media eyes bestowed special attention to how the legislation was received in the United States. The spectre of the Canada–US relationship loomed large as the main interrogation was about the impact the new regulation would have on bilateral relations, with possible spillover effects on other files.

Ultimately, the crisis subsided, with no new transit and no effort on the part of the Americans to challenge the Arctic Waters Pollution Prevention Act (AWPPA). Negotiations on a multilateral agreement setting maritime boundaries and regulations proved to be less of an appealing story for the media to cover than the two Manhattan transits. Until a new sovereignty crisis erupted, that is.

The 1985 Polar Sea transit

Another incident 15 years later returned the Arctic to the front of the national stage. Three (3) newspapers were studied (*The Globe and Mail*, *Toronto Star* and *Montreal Gazette*) thanks to more comprehensive archival access. From the first editorial published on the issue on 13 June 1985 to the end of December of that same year, 170 articles were published containing the mention "Polar Sea," of which 123 had the Polar Sea incident as main focus[5]. The 1985 Polar Sea crisis exhibited different dynamics. Instead of two different episodes of intense media coverage, only one such instance could be observed, making the 1985 transit a much more intense albeit short convulsion. As can be seen in Figure 1.2, the bulk of media coverage concerning this episode peaked in early-mid August, before receding quickly after the Minister of External Affairs Commons statement on Arctic sovereignty on 10 September.

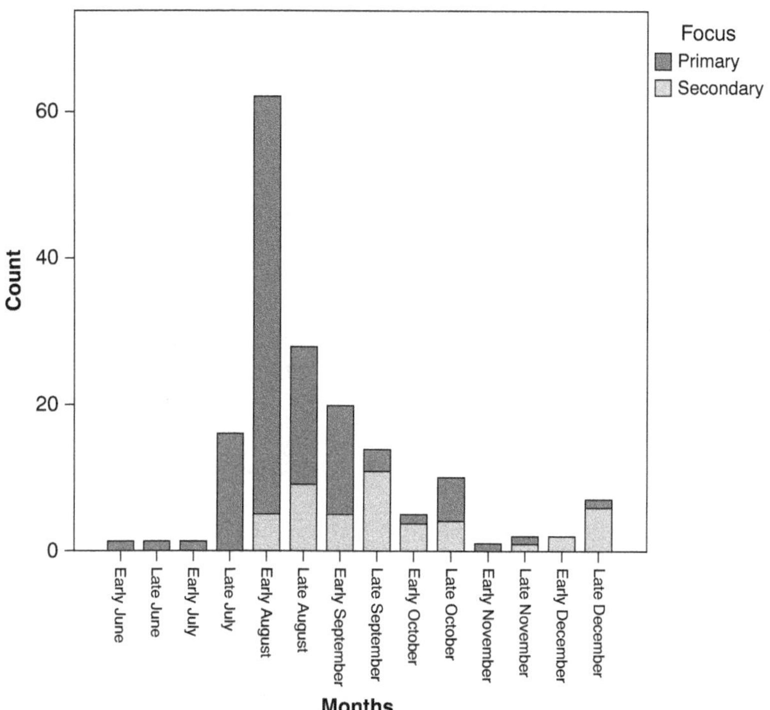

Figure 1.2 Number of news articles, editorials, and letters to the editor mentioning the Polar Sea incident in the *Montreal Gazette*, *Globe and Mail*, and *Toronto Star* by time of month.

The 1969 incident had left its mark, albeit in an indirect fashion: it prompted Canadian scholars to devote more attention to Arctic issues. International law experts conducted studies to clarify issues and debates on the legal status of the Northwest Passage (NWP). Both the introduction of the AWPPA and the efforts leading to the signature of the United Nations Convention on the Law of the Sea (UNCLOS) in 1982 contributed to this increased scholarly interest from an international law perspective. Donat Pharand, from the University of Ottawa, Ron Macdonald, from Dalhousie, and Gerald Morris, from the University of Toronto, were good examples of this. Other academics, like Franklyn Griffiths or Harriet Critchley, concentrated their efforts on geopolitical or strategic considerations.

This expertise was almost absent from media coverage in 1969, except for a handful of editorials written by academics. In fact, scholars were the first to ring the alarm bell at the onset of the 1985 transit. In total, 21 texts were either signed by or quoted Arctic experts during the entire time period studied. Half of these interventions were done during the first month and a half of the crisis, or before its apex. Out of the first 16 articles or editorials published on the transit, 8 either were written by or contained a contribution from an Arctic scholar. An active and vocal academic community was at the forefront. Griffiths, for example, presented a balanced description of the transit:

> Canadians ought not to assume that the Polar Sea poses a make-or-break challenge to Arctic sovereignty. We appear to be faced with a carefully calibrated move, not with an attempt to undo the Canadian position in a single act.
>
> (Griffiths, June 13 1985: p. 7)

Although not in an overly alarmist fashion, Griffiths nonetheless predicted a hot summer related to the Arctic file in Ottawa. Implicitly, his opinion ran counter to governmental messaging. The Conservative government repeated *ad nauseam* that the transit did not "pose a threat to Canada's claim of sovereignty in the Arctic waters," trusting their US counterparts that the transit was solely to save time and expense (Sallot, June 21 1985: p. 8).

Another striking contrast with the 1969 crisis is that civil society played an active role before, during and after the transit. The activism of regular citizens voicing their opinion constituted a significant difference with the first incident. In 1969, only 4% of the texts mentioning the Manhattan were letters to the editor, while this very proportion tripled during the 1985 crisis[6]. Most of the letters expressed plain outrage or complained about the overly permissive and hesitant attitude of the Mulroney government.

As far as organized civil society was concerned, two groups stood out. The first, Inuit voices, were given a tribune in 1985, in contrast to the 1969 incident when they were made virtually absent from media coverage. In the case of the Polar Sea transit, the Inuit Tapirisat of Canada representatives were interviewed many times by journalists, as they voiced Inuit concerns about the upcoming American voyage. The organization shared similar concerns with Arctic scholars:

> the transit constitutes a challenge to Canadian sovereignty and jurisdiction that ultimately could have far-reaching implications for effective environmental control in the Arctic.
>
> (Innuksuk cited in Platiel, July 10 1985: p. 17)

The issue of protection of Inuit rights and customs was also an integral part of the arguments to oppose the transit in many editorials. In fact, Inuit representatives and points of view proved to be more widespread than academic ones, and were found in 27 documents.

The Council of Canadians also proved to be a central actor in the crisis. Founded in March 1985, the nationalist group gave a new impetus to the public outcry with direct actions. During the 1969 crisis, only one organized civil society group (an association of business interests) was reported in the *Globe and Mail*. The Council of Canadians mounted an expedition to meet the Polar Sea in order to directly deliver their message to US personnel on board the ship. Unable to reach them, they resigned themselves to drop on or near the vessel a canister containing a Canadian flag and messages of protest. The organization attracted considerable media attention at the height of the crisis, from 6 to 10 August, immediately before the Polar Sea entered Canadian waters on August 11 (Marotte, August 12 1985: p. 5). This heightened media coverage preceded a reorientation of Canada's Arctic policy.

Indeed, it was first reported on 2 August that the Ministry of External Affairs might launch an in-depth review of the country's Arctic policy (Yaffe, August 2 1985, p. 1). The story made it to the front page of the *Globe and Mail*; no official confirmation followed these rumours. Subsequently, on 11 August, Joe Clark admitted asking "Canadian shipping firms to provide design specifications to build its own icebreaker," a sign of the statement that was to come in early September (Clark cited in Marotte, August 12 1985, p. 5). However, Clark continued minimizing the gravity of the incident, blaming the media for blowing the story of the transit out of proportion. The voyage was instead for the minister "a strong assertion of Canadian sovereignty" (Clark cited in Marotte, August 12 1985, p. 5). As can be observed in Figure 1.3, intense media coverage preceded policy change. In fact, both governmental initiatives were made public at the end of the two busiest weeks (week of 29 July and 5 August) of the crisis.

The Canadian position definitely shifted on August 21 when Clark announced upcoming measures to strengthen Canadian Arctic sovereignty. Clark made it clear that Canada would not refer the dispute to the International Court of Justice, instead alluding that material capabilities to patrol and control the Canadian Arctic should be a priority. Prime Minister Brian Mulroney followed up on his minister's remarks the next day, as he called any suggestion that the NWP did not belong to Canada an "unfriendly act" and added that the Government of Canada would continue to ensure that it belonged to Canada (Mulroney cited in The Gazette, August 23 1985, p. B1).

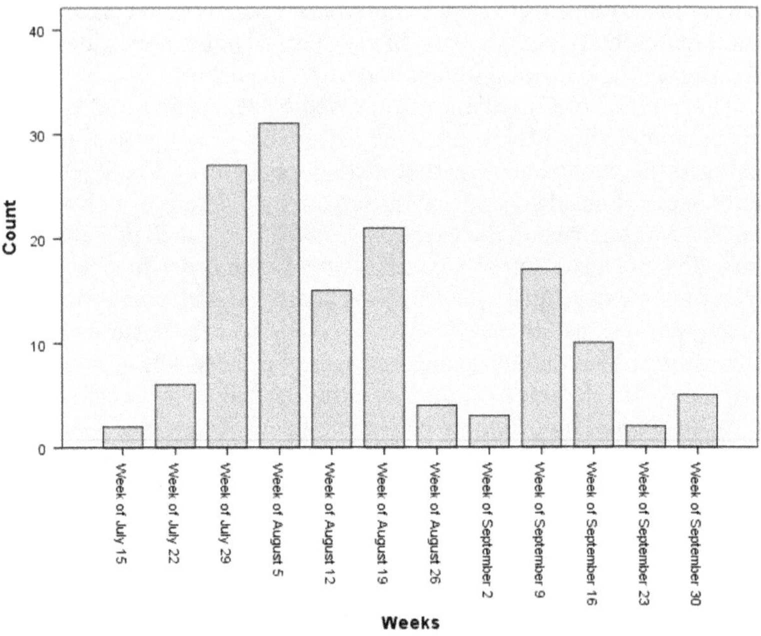

Figure 1.3 Number of news articles, editorials, and letters to the editor mentioning the Polar Sea in the *Montreal Gazette*, *Globe and Mail*, and *Toronto Star* by weeks, from July 15 to September 30.

Contrary to the 1969 crisis, the announcement of future measures did not significantly impact media attention. In fact, both the *Globe and Mail* and the *Toronto Star* published editorials after Clark's comments supporting more concrete actions rather than vague allusions: these included drawing straight baselines, financing the construction of a class 8 icebreaker, building radar stations, and increasing the presence of Canadian Forces in the region.

Media presence only receded after Joe Clark's statement in front of the House of Commons on 10 September. In his address, the Minister of external Affairs laid down the concrete initiatives that his government was going to pursue in the future to support Arctic sovereignty, including drawing straight baselines and purchasing an icebreaker.

The Polar Sea and the Canada–US relationship

Media attention towards the Polar Sea incident was remarkably different that the media coverage of the Manhattan transits. For one, no journalist was aboard to report on the day-to-day progress of the voyage, nor did the Polar Sea represent a scientific endeavour or commercial enterprise that could yield fundamental economic benefits. Very few developments worthy of reporting even occurred during the transit, with the exception of a short-lived controversy (only from 1 to 3 August) hinting at the possibility that the Polar Sea might carry out scientific tests while in Canadian waters[7].

Hesitation predominantly characterized the initial governmental approach both in 1969 and 1985. The timing of both transits, in the month of August, seemed to also catch decision-makers off guard. This period usually was a slow-news period both in the media and government circles: the governmental apparatus had already started working on many priorities and concrete measures, as can be deduced from the flurry of announcements made in September 1985 (on the US Strategic Defence Initiative (SDI), or the creation of national parks or new ethical rules, for example).

The most significant difference between the two crises rested in the nature of the Canada–US relationship. The 1969 Manhattan incident brought forth an emphasis on the possibility of a continental energy policy. The main issue frame on this incident was to understand how the Manhattan transit could impact the integration of energy resources between both North American partners. A successful transit would have meant that the USA had the capacity to bypass Canada in order to get oil resources to market. However, this remained more of a peripheral discussion, a secondary consideration of a sectoral nature. The nature of the Canada–US relationship was also quite stable and predictable, with no fundamental change in sight[8].

The landslide victory of the Conservative party of Canada in the 1984 general elections a year prior to the Polar Sea crisis did not favour the Mulroney government. In fact, the Prime Minister displayed a different attitude towards the US partner, advocating for a strengthening of the special relationship between both countries. The Shamrock Summit, in March 1985, constituted a powerful symbol of this rapprochement, with images of Prime Minister Mulroney and President Reagan singing together making headlines.

The strategy was a gamble: a better entente with the USA had to pay off in the minds of Canadians. In this context, the transit of the Polar Sea and the unwillingness of the American government to ask permission and recognize Canadian jurisdiction over the NWP were seen as signs that the Mulroney approach was failing. If a closer personal relationship with the president and a greater willingness to cooperate with the US administration did not make the USA respect Canadian sensitivities and key interests in the Arctic, what was the point in pursuing such a path?

Fundamental issues in the Canada–US relationship were around the corner. The USA was pressing Canada to fully participate in research for the SDI (also known as Star Wars). More importantly, talks were already at an advanced stage for starting formal negotiations on a Canada–US Free Trade Agreement. The polemic also generated speculations about possible linkages between Arctic sovereignty and the upcoming free trade negotiations, leading Prime Minister Mulroney to state the following: "certain issues such as [...] Arctic sovereignty will not be on the table when Canada sits down to discuss freer trade with the United States" (Mulroney cited in *Globe and Mail*, September 16 1985: p. 3).

The crisis had a lasting effect, and this, months after the Polar Sea arrived at dock. In fact, 70% of all texts mentioning the Polar Sea after Clark's Commons statement did not focus primarily on Arctic sovereignty, but rather on the evolution of the Canada–US bilateral relationship.

Agenda setting and past sovereignty crises

Media played an important role in both the 1969 and 1985 crises to set the agenda, although news outlets were helped by external factors. However, the approach adopted by the Government of Canada also had an impact on the intensity and duration of each crisis. Legislation introduced in the Fall of 1969 required debate before being officialized; it also contributed to a second wave of media coverage in the Winter of 1970. Furthermore, political parties were instrumental during the 1969 Manhattan episode at pressing government to provide the Canadian populace with specific answers. This in turn brought government to push its political messaging more intensely so as to counteract opposition parties. The ruling Liberal Party was caught by surprise, with Liberal MPs disagreeing publically about the best course of action. Opposition MPs were also quite skilful into insisting on the second Manhattan transit in the winter/spring 1970.

During the 1985 crisis, Joe Clark's statement had for effect to calm public clamour. The initiatives or investments announced were not of a legislative nature, thus ensuring that the debate did not drag on for weeks or months. Key announcements by the acting government were done at the end of the two weeks that observed the most media intensity. Hence, the media performed agenda setting during this crucial time period. However, on a longer timeline, the fact that the American government, through the voice of the US ambassador to Canada Thomas Niles, "could understand why Canadians were unhappy" certainly helped the situation in 1985. Niles admitted further that the transit was "just not worth the aggravation" (*Globe and Mail*, September 30 1985: p. 4). The attitude of the Nixon government was not so apologetic in 1969, with the USA opposing the legislation adopted by their Canadian counterparts.

The Polar Sea incident was put on a pedestal by the activism of many different actors, with Inuit groups, the Council of Canadians and political parties being the most active. Thus, the media was not working in a void; media outlets required other social and political actors to intervene and take ownership of the issue in order to devote time and efforts to these developments. Editorials and letters to the editor are tools with which newspapers spread their opinions; news articles, on the other hand, feed off concrete real-life actions and developments by the political elite and/or organized civil society. In fact, it would seem that the latter turned out to be an essential ingredient for fostering crises in both 1969 and 1985.

In both sovereignty episodes, the use of different issue frames was central to heightened media interest: the presence of multiple angles to both stories contributed to significant media attention. Beside the Arctic sovereignty angle, the 1969 Manhattan voyage stirred questions about continental energy policies, world shipping dynamics and environmental protection. The fact that the Manhattan transit was a precedent, seen as a scientific accomplishment, made for a richer story providing day-to-day coverage. Journalists on board of the John A. Macdonald icebreaker provided daily coverage and framed the voyage in the vocabulary of expeditions of the past and explorers.

In comparison, a first glance at the 1985 crisis did not garner as many angles. An icebreaker did not spark as many stories on environmental protection, international shipping or energy considerations as the voyage of a tanker. The Arctic sovereignty frame dominated media coverage, but the broader Canada–US relationship was also an integral part of the coverage. Important questions, on defence matters or free trade, rendered the crisis more salient; the crisis was framed as a test and precautionary tale of Mulroney's conciliatory approach towards the American ally.

Notes

1 Evidently, this process also required filtering out the many unrelated stories that such a keyword has generated.

2 Many other articles mentioned the Manhattan transit but with a different topic as main focus. For example, many articles discussed continental energy policy or covered the shipping industry in general.

3 For instance, in the 13 September editorial, the newspaper praised the government for not succumbing to ultranationalism and chauvinism.
4 For example, Trudeau referred to Arctic waters as low seas and Canadian waters rather than territorial or internal waters.
5 It is interesting to note, however, that the number of news articles published in the *Globe and Mail* during the 1985 controversy was of only 73. This figure is lower than the number of articles published in the same newspaper on a similar time period (roughly 6 months) during the Manhattan crisis.
6 Of course, it is impossible to know whether the newspapers received more letters from their readership about the voyage or if they selected letters that resonated with their opinion of the crisis. Only first-hand testimonies from people working on the editorial teams of these newspapers at the time could provide a satisfying answer.
7 The possibility that the US navy would carry out scientific tests underwater was first reported on 2 August. However, US officials clearly defused the situation by publicly stating that no scientific test would be carried out over while the icebreaker was in Canadian waters.
8 Of course, this was before the economic crises hit the developed world in the 1970s.

References

Crane, David. September 3 1969. Ceding of Passage Rights Likely in Ottawa Claim to Arctic Waters. *Globe and Mail*, p. B1.

Globe and Mail. July 15 1969. Professor-like Trudeau Replies to Briefs, Wins Applause, a Few Cheers in Churchill, p. 4.

Globe and Mail. June 28 1969. No Claim to Islands, p. 11.

Globe and Mail. August 29 1969. MPs to Greet Manhattan During Inspection of Northern Waterway, p. 25.

Globe and Mail. September 5 1969. The Master Sails Elsewhere, p. 6.

Globe and Mail. September 13 1969. Guard on the Jewel Case, p. 6.

Globe and Mail. February 18 1970. In the Arctic the Wrong Man Is Meek, p. 6.

Globe and Mail. February 25 1970. PM Refuses Statement, p. B2.

Globe and Mail. September 16 1985. PM Says SDI, Arctic Taboo at Trade Talks, p. 3.

Globe and Mail. September 30 1985. Social Programs Not at Risk, U.S. Envoy Says, p. 4.

Griffiths, Franklyn. June 13 1985. Arctic Authority at Stake. *Globe and Mail*, p. 7.

Marotte, Bertrand. August 12 1985. Icebreaker Leaves Canadian Waters. *Globe and Mail*, p. 5.

Newman, Donald. February 14 1970. Trudeau, U.S. Making Secret Compromise on Arctic, MP Says. *Globe and Mail*, p. 4.

Newman, Donald. February 20 1970. Sharp Make Claim to Arctic Waters. *Globe and Mail*, p. 1.

Platiel, Rudy. July 10 1985. Voyage of a U.S. Ship a Violation of Sovereignty, Inuit Fear. *Globe and Mail*, p. 17.

Sallot, Jeff. June 21 1985. Northwest Passage Sovereignty Disputed – Diplomatic Icebergs Stew Voyage. *Globe and Mail*, p. 8.

The Gazette. August 23 1985. Our Arctic Claim Not in Doubt: PM, Montreal, p. B1.

Wanta, Wayne, Golan, Guy and Lee, Cheolhan. 2004. Agenda Setting and International News: Media Influence on Public Perceptions of Foreign Nations. *Journalism and Mass Communication Quarterly*, volume 81, issue 2: pp. 364–77.

Watkins, Lyndon. August 28 1969. Drifting Barge May Endanger Manhattan. *Globe and Mail*, p. B2.

Yaffe, Barbara. August 2 1985. "Must Get Act Together" – Canada to Launch Sovereignty Review. *Globe and Mail*, p. 1.

2 Time to ring the alarm bell?

> Consider how much pure water you could load on a tanker. There's (sic) a lot of places in the world where pure fresh water is hard to come by, and a lot of money could be made by someone sending a ship to the Canadian Arctic where there is a lot of good water to be had.
>
> – Col. (ret.) Pierre Leblanc (cited in Struzik, November 5 2000)

The years 1969 and 1985 are crucial for Canada's Arctic sovereignty claims. Both years generated challenges stemming from an unauthorized transit by an American vessel: first with the tanker *Manhattan* (1969), followed by the icebreaker *Polar Sea* (1985). Both crises provoked great levels of public outcry.

These events are labelled as crises by virtue of causing spontaneous outbursts of public interest towards Arctic sovereignty. These types of events are ephemeral in nature: they come and go, attracting popular attention before subsiding. The Canadian Arctic experienced such fate, with various measures undertaken to strengthen Arctic sovereignty; in fact, these were announced with great fervour in 1970 and in the years following the 1985 crisis, only to later fall victim to budget cuts. The 1988 Canada–US Arctic Co-operation Agreement played a pivotal role in preventing additional tensions and disputes: as an "agree to disagree" accord, both countries settled on a practical arrangement without resolving the core disagreement on the legal status of the Northwest Passage (NWP). The arrangement stipulated that the United States agreed to ask permission to their Canadian counterparts before transiting a governmental vessel through the NWP. In return, Canada agreed to always grant permission to the Americans. This was deemed by both states as a compromise that would not cause prejudice to the legal position defended by either country.

Free from new sovereignty crises, the Government of Canada adopted a different approach to Canadian Arctic Security and Sovereignty (CASS) in the 1990s, one that focused on the development of a regional governance framework alongside other Arctic states. The frequency of Arctic surveillance patrols by the Canadian Forces (CF) declined, reaching a low of one annual flight by the mid-1990s. In the words of then Foreign Affairs minister Lloyd Axworthy,

> In terms of today's world, one of the most important ways of (asserting sovereignty over the Arctic) is not through the old traditional means of sending an icebreaker [...] That was ... in the old days. We're moving into a new age.
>
> (Axworthy cited in *Toronto Star*, June 9 2000)

In retrospect, the 1990s seemed uneventful for CASS. Liberal international institutionalism and human security, emphasizing on socio-economic and environmental concerns rather than military ones, was the dominant approach to Arctic affairs. The business-as-usual policy to count on ice to prevent further incursions in Canadian Arctic waters prevailed, as multi-year ice made the region difficult to navigate and represented a hazard for maritime commercial interests. It should be noted that Canada was perceived as ready to ripe the peace dividend assumed to be prevalent as a result of the end of the Cold War.

In this context, impending global warming acted as a new variable susceptible of impacting Canadian interests in the region. The "susceptible" variable of the equation constituted the crux of the debate: would global warming threaten CASS? Was it time to ring the alarm bell? As the quote introducing this chapter suggests, some experts answered by an apprehensive yes to these questions. But were they dominant?

Global warming as a threat?

The academic debate around this question centred on two key scholars: Rob Huebert and Franklyn Griffiths. Huebert and Griffiths exchanged views through articles published in the *International Journal* in 2003; their exchange came to be known as the sovereignty-on-thinning-ice debate. Griffiths offered an answer to Huebert's position, which was published in the *Canadian Foreign Policy Journal*. The main disagreement focused on the extent of the impacts that global warming would have on Canadian Arctic claims.

First, Griffiths deconstructed the sovereignty-on-thinning-ice thesis, questioning the core assumption that global warming would bring "relatively speedy and undifferentiated ice-cover reduction" (2003: p. 263). In his mind, the intrinsic uncertainty of the ice melt would make the prospect of transiting through the NWP an unlikely scenario; risks of accident and delays would still be elevated, making shipping companies reluctant to go through the NWP.

Griffiths further opposed the alarmism of some scholars and policy makers alike who stated that Canadian Arctic sovereignty was under threat. Rather than apocalyptic assessments, a more moderate evaluation would be in order: "Canada should start preparing more actively for intermittent commercial transits in conformity with Canadian law. But it does not report new danger to Canada's Arctic sovereignty" (Griffiths, 2003: p. 269). Overinflated assessments of CASS threats would orient Canadian Arctic policy in the wrong direction, leading the country to invest in assets or implement measures that would not be in synch with reality.

In opposition to Griffiths, Huebert argued that a warming Arctic would "become a more accessible Arctic for the international community. It is this greater accessibility that will test Canada's ability to ensure that this region remains protected and promoted for all Canadians, including those that call it home" (Huebert, 2003: p. 295). He supported the idea that melting Arctic ice was creating an urgent problem and brought forth challenges to Canada's Arctic sovereignty. While he agreed that reputable shipping companies were not risk prone, a more open NWP would attract "risk-oriented shipping companies" and "substandard vessels" in Canadian Arctic waters (Huebert, 2003: pp. 302–4). For Huebert, this fear was heightened by the possibility that "only a few international voyages taken without Canadian permission may be enough to render our (Canada's sovereignty) claims invalid" (305). These fears were presented as even more urgent in nature considering the limited surveillance, control, and enforcement assets deployed by the Government of Canada in its Arctic.

Thus, the sovereignty-on-thinning-ice debate presented the reader with two radically different narratives. The first of these narratives presented Canada's Arctic sovereignty as relatively secured, untouched for the most part by the upcoming ice melt. Canadian sovereignty was not under attack, putting in question the relevance of adopting a defence-of-sovereignty approach rooted in military expenditures to enforce Canadian sovereignty over its Arctic. In reference to Stéphane Roussel's imagery, the Arctic was not under siege (2010) and was not likely to be in the near future. In turn, solutions could be declined on a long-term horizon, with a focus on enhancing the role played by Inuit to assert Canadian sovereignty.

This narrative was also spread by governmental officials. The 2000 Northern Dimension of Canada's Foreign Policy stressed the potential of cooperation rather than the potential dangers and perils unleashed by global warming. Priorities ranged from strengthening the Arctic Council (which creation was spearheaded by Canada) to deepening bilateral relations with Russia or improving northern trade and education opportunities (Department of Foreign Affairs, 2000). Threats were not so much framed as consequences of increased mobility, but rather as transnational and global environmental menaces. Hence, transboundary environmental issues such as climate change, the presence of persistent organic pollutants in Arctic waters, and the safe management of nuclear waste in the Russian Arctic were front and centre in this policy document.

The second narrative, defended by Huebert, put forward a darker evaluation of CASS. Dangers and challenges were looming; the ice melt would only produce increased mobility, which in turn would bring forth challenges to Canada's claim on the NWP. A more open Arctic also meant a variety of potential actors getting involved, be it state or non-state. This assessment presented these threats as imminent and inevitable unless decisive actions were taken. These actions had to guarantee that Canada could cast effective control over its Arctic waters, requiring greater assets to enforce Canadian laws and ensure surveillance. This second interpretation could be charged with being alarmist given that the menaces were constructed in grave terms, predicting that not taking them seriously could spell disastrous consequences, namely, that Canada could "lose substantial control over regions of the north by its delayed action" (Huebert, 2003: p. 297).

This second perspective was also articulated in governmental documents, albeit later in the time period studied. The 2005 Government of Canada's international statement *Pride and Influence in the World* recuperated some of these concerns. It was estimated that increased activity in the region would create "long-term security implications" and "asymmetrical threats" including "sovereignty and environmental protection, organized crime, and people and drug smuggling" (Department of National Defence, 2005: p. 17).

Hence, two clear positions could be deciphered from 2000 to 2005, thus describing Arctic reality in different terms. The media was a preferred terrain where academics, public servants, civil society leaders, and political elites could popularize their understanding of what the Arctic was confronted to. The media acted as a vehicle to diffuse ideas to a broader audience, a public venue for scholars to widely spread their opinions, in contrast to their messages being restricted to a specialized audience in academic conferences or to a limited readership in scholarly journals. Hence, the relevance of the sovereignty-on-thinning-ice debate lied in the diffusion of its ideas in the public sphere. Media, especially newspapers, often relied on experts to provide informed opinions and assessments in journalistic articles. These journalistic reports were particularly persuasive documents as they aspired to norms of objectivity and neutrality; it is easy to read these texts and interpret them as objective descriptions of reality.

Hence, experts are pivotal actors as they provide opinions or comments that journalists cannot typically express. The selection of experts cited in newspapers articles proves to be a key element of analysis; this selection bias may be caused by pragmatic (expert availability, willingness to participate) and/or subjective (expert opinion fitting with framing utilized by journalists, general narrative of the article) factors.

The experts most consulted by reporters are academics. This category is particularly important in regards to Arctic issues because scholars are quite active in the public discussion and policy debate about the Arctic region. Therefore, their influence is not limited to the academic community; decision-makers and the public pay attention to their opinions. As Huebert put it, Griffiths' public interventions "have often played an integral role in prodding the government to actually 'do' something in the north" (Huebert, 2003: p. 296). Other than Griffiths, Arctic academics in Canada have been particularly active, advocating publicly that more should be done on Arctic issues. Academics are still considered the "most important securitizing actor (sic) in the Arctic sovereignty debate" (Chater, 2012: p. 834). Hence, it would seem logical to begin by analyzing the prevalence of academic opinions in the media.

Experts and journalists

So as to evaluate the media input of the academic community, a study of all journalistic articles published in 15 Canadian newspapers[1] using the key terms "Arctic sovereignty" and "Arctic security", was undertaken. These newspapers were gathered using the Canadian Major Dailies database. The timeline studied ranged from 9 June 2000 to 19 April 2005, or between the day following the announcement of the *Northern Dimension of Canadian Foreign Policy* and the following major policy paper dealing with Arctic sovereignty, the 2005 international policy statement, *A Role of Pride and Influence in the World.*

Overall, 70 journalistic articles were found. Media attention followed an uneven pattern during this time period, as illustrated in Figure 2.1.

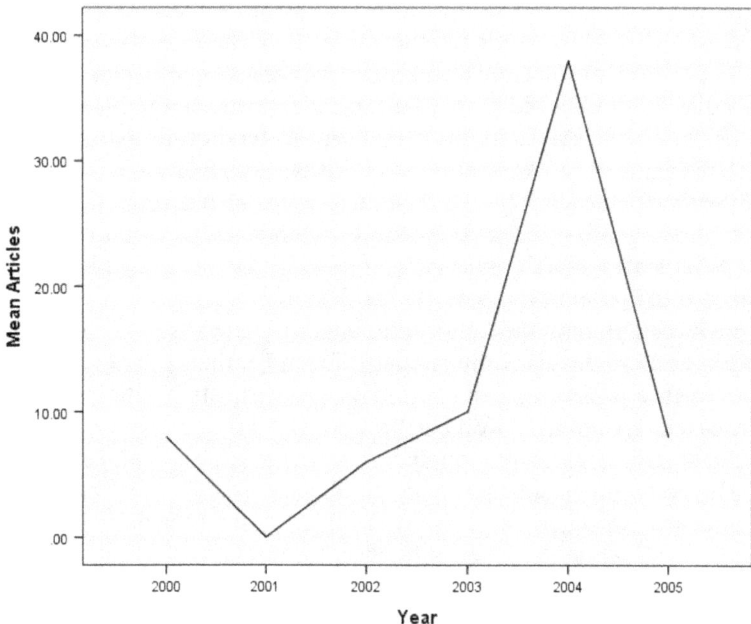

Figure 2.1 Distribution by year of journalistic articles on Arctic sovereignty and security issues from June 2000 to April 2005.

Media attention peaked in 2004 but it would seem that overall attention increased, considering that 2005 only covered four months (January–April). The Hans island dispute in July/August of that same year would have engendered a clear increase in numbers. It should also be noted that this heightened coverage is not merely the result of one or two newspapers trying to emphasize Arctic issues; newspapers with diverse geographical distributions, ownership, and scope (regional or national) published articles on Arctic issues.

Sovereignty represented the predominant term of reference; close to 85% of all articles dealt with Arctic sovereignty rather than Arctic security. This comes as no surprise when one pays attention to the vocabulary used in editorials written during this same time period. Based on this author's studies conducted on editorials, a focus on sovereignty outweighed by far one on security (Landriault, 2013, pp. 89–102).

Further, we also know that, among the two main protagonists in the sovereignty-on-thinning-ice debate, Huebert's vision was more widespread. In many cases, these editorials went even further, explicitly defending the use-it-or-lose-it principle. In fact, the idea that Canada will lose its Arctic to other countries if the federal government does not invest to occupy its territory was mentioned in close to 45% of editorials published from 2000 to 2005 (Landriault, 2013: p. 96). This raised the stakes as the possibility of territorial disintegration was presented as a likely outcome if the level of investments observed at the time persisted. The Canadian Arctic was also described as a unitary, homogenous space; the entire Canadian Arctic could be seized by other states, in a domino fashion in which losing a tiny part of the space could potentially spark further losses.

Can such gloomy predictions be found in journalistic articles? Did experts articulate this vision publicly? To answer these queries, it would make sense to focus on the two main protagonists' media presence, Franklyn Griffiths and Rob Huebert. Thus, all the passages where one of these two scholars were quoted or paraphrased were tallied.

Huebert's media involvement far outweighed Griffiths' exposure; the former was cited or paraphrased in 12 different articles totalling 1,295 words while the latter only once, for a total of 51 words. As expected, the nature of Huebert's quoted passages closely resembled his sovereignty-on-thinning-ice position. In 7 of these 12 articles, he raised the possibility of an impending sovereignty challenge against which Canada is ill-equipped to win. However, he was adamant at playing down the risk posed by military threats, calling them "negligible" compared to sovereignty disputes (VanderKlippe, September 19 2004: p. A3). These passages also displayed a "use it or lose it" rationale, in which Canada, by not exercising control over its Arctic territories, would inevitably suffer a loss of territory: "In protecting their own interests, Huebert said other countries will take over Canada's territory – and it will be Canada's fault" (Rempel, 2003: p. A4).

At first glance, the media seemed to favour one framing over the other. However, explanations for this favouritism are not straightforward; the two academic experts had radically different visions of their role in relation with the media. Based on separate interviews conducted with both Huebert and Griffiths, diametrically different perspectives on the media emerged. In Griffiths' case, the main focus of his work was to exchange with officials and decision-makers so as to come up with better, sounder policies. Journalists were often perceived by Griffiths as poorly informed on Arctic issues. Further, the media was perceived as epiphenomenal (manifestations of other phenomenon), and as merely taking part in the business of selling worry-type stories.

On the other hand, Huebert felt a need, as an academic, to go beyond the classroom and share his expertise with the general public; the media acted as a vehicle to achieve this objective and involvement in the media was perceived as a responsibility. It is interesting to note that Huebert shares some of Griffiths' take on the limited potential of the media as an independent phenomenon. Huebert described the media's potential effect on policies as indirect and punctual, only effective when a statement was often repeated or when it supported what people in power wanted to hear. However, this did not keep him from repeatedly sharing his thoughts in the media.

The fact that Huebert's media presence far outweighed Griffiths' is not informative of the opinions expressed by Huebert in these journalistic articles. Hence, one must focus on his contributions to assess if he defended alarmist assessments[2] about the state of Canadian Arctic Sovereignty and Security (CASS).

The evidence does not yield a straightforward answer. Out of the 12 times his input was solicited, 7 can be labelled as pessimistic or as predicting sovereignty challenges. These predictions were expressed mostly in the first few years of the time period studied, the 2000–2003 period, which accounted for five of the seven pessimistic predictions. For example, Huebert predicted that the Arctic sovereignty issue could "blow up" as a result of a mostly uncooperative Bush administration (cited in Appelbe, August 27 2002: p. A16). Other quotes include asserting that Canada is "ill-prepared to win the next sovereignty battle" (Farrell, September 18 2002: p. I10), or listing emerging threats facing the Canadian Arctic:

> with less ice and new opportunities for shipping, you have the prospect of environmental and military threats, the potential for new smuggling routes to be opened up, and an unprotected back door for illegal immigration.
>
> (Struzik, November 5 2000: p. E7)

The central arguments forming the basis of Huebert's sovereignty-on-thinning-ice position are formulated in the aforementioned passages, highlighting the heightened value of the Arctic region in terms of natural resources, and especially in terms of the potential it holds for commercial shipping companies. Increased interest means increased challenges to Canada's position, worsened by the inadequate level of preparedness of the Canadian government to ensure proper surveillance and presence in its Arctic. In relation to the use-it-or-lose-it principle often vocalized in editorials during this time period, Huebert definitely advocated for its first component ("use-it") by criticizing the poor level of resources devoted to affirming Canada's sovereignty. However, the "lose-it" component was not explicitly stated by Huebert; while pessimistic about the challenges the country was confronted to, the possibility of losing the region was not frequently voiced by Huebert. He was quoted in a single article explicitly expressing the idea of a loss of sovereignty.

Additionally, it should be emphasized that not all of Huebert's quoted passages were pessimistic. In fact, five contributions were categorized as not pessimistic or alarmist, with two even downplaying the presence of threats. For example, he qualified military threats potentially present in the North as "negligible" (VanderKlippe, September 19 2004: p. A3). In other articles, Huebert complained about the poor material state of the CF, without making alarmist predictions for CASS. This in turn yielded a nuanced portrait of the leading academic voice on CASS. It must be underlined that Huebert and Griffiths were not the only university experts sought after. A great diversity of experts was consulted during this time period. Table 2.1 offers a glimpse of these multiple points of views.

Table 2.1 Academics quoted or paraphrased in journalistic articles published in 15 Canadian newspapers from 2000 to 2005

Name	*Number of articles*	*Number of words quoted or paraphrased*
Rob Huebert	12	1295
Barry Prentice	6	1116
Gerry Kenney	6	1021
Donald McRae	5	245
Christopher Sands	4	743
Martin Shadwick	3	137
Louis Fortier	2	129
Tom Hutchinson	1	45
Peter Haydon	1	141
Clifford Hickey	1	131
George Sofko	1	124
Andrew Weaver	1	14
Duncan McDowell	1	189
P. Whitney Lackenbauer	1	18
Jozef Wiktor	1	33
William Morrison	1	25
David Bercuson	1	21
Franklyn Griffiths	1	51
Morris Maduro	1	34
Michael Behiel	1	246

Overall, academics are the most frequently solicited external experts by journalists. However, our definition of experts must not be solely limited to scholars. Indeed, a broader take on expertise expands the scope beyond the academia. Public servants and civil society representatives are also precious resources for journalists. Indeed, participants in the former group may be considered experts, as they provide specific knowledge (think the Canadian Ice Service) or on-the-ground know-how (e.g., CF personnel) while civil society actors represent the voices and interests of specific segments of the Canadian population (e.g., the Inuit Circumpolar Council). Political elites, namely, politicians, also make claims about security threats. Journalists have sought the insights of these individuals to comment on and share their opinions on Arctic issues.

Hence, the data analysis was broadened so as to consider all external sources cited or paraphrased in the reporting articles gathered. Instead of being limited to the 21 academic experts listed previously, the expert opinions expressed by 86 different individuals, each coming from different walks of life, must now be accounted for (see Table 2.2).

Two types of contributors stand out in this list, and for opposite reasons. The first, civil society representatives, are quasi absent from these articles. Hence, Inuit voices were not often represented, rendering exposition to Inuit perspectives on security and sovereignty issues scarce. Outspoken Inuit leader Sheila Watt-Cloutier accounted for more than 55% of these civil society interventions. Inuit were also represented in the military personnel category as members of the Canadian Rangers, a sub-component of the Canadian Armed Forces Reserve primarily composed of Inuit. The second type of contributors, military personnel, was often solicited by journalists to supplement

Table 2.2 External actors quoted or paraphrased and the size of their contributions in 15 Canadian newspapers from June 2000 to April 2005

Type of contributor	*Number of different contributors*	*Number of passages quoted or paraphrased*	*Number of words quoted or paraphrased*
Academic	21	52	5,782
Military personnel[3]	29	49	4,062
Political representatives[4]	18	37	3,520
Bureaucracy	13	15	878
Civil society	5	7	551
Total	86	160	14,793

the storyline. This change exhibited a reflection of the reengagement of the Canadian military in patrolling and ensuring surveillance of the North.

In fact, starting in 2002, the CF reinstated large-scale deployments combining air, maritime, and land personnel, known as operation NARWHAL. The sovereignty patrols created much buzz around sovereignty issues; they acted as singular events around which journalistic interest coalesced and developed compelling stories. Articles written to cover operation NARWHAL where, on average, lengthier than all other articles combined (858 words against 776 words, respectively).

Two narratives proved to be dominant in the pieces focusing on sovereignty operations. One set of reports used the operation as an opportunity to brush a portrayal of the state of Canadian sovereignty claims, listing possible dangers and evaluating potential policy responses. Broad historical reviews, from Diefenbaker to Chrétien, were widespread to describe the evolution of these claims and policies. The second set of reports focused on the Rangers patrol and the sovereignty operations conducted in April, which were more minor in scope. These generated a particular type of stories, taking the form of a travelogue of sorts, focusing on the harsh Arctic environment and particularities related to running sovereignty patrols in such an inhospitable landscape. In some ways, these reports resembled 19th century explorer tales. This connection was highlighted in one of these articles:

> Not far from Alert lie the Arctic graves of sailors and explorers whose role in daring quests to map and discover new lands ended in agonizing deaths.
>
> (VanderKlippe, April 17 2004: p. A17)

Two articles written by journalist Nathan VanderKlippe in April 2004 and January 2005, exemplified perfectly this tendency as rugged environment and adversity were front and centre of the narrative:

> It is a land of spectacular scenery: low-lying wooded foothills tucked before snow-capped mountains, access by a narrow road cuts along cliffs and frozen rivers. Yet it is also harsh and cold, and for the Rangers, the object of being here in the middle of a January deep-freeze is to hone traditional and military skills that could be called on in a time of conflict or emergency.
>
> (VanderKlippe, January 23 2005: p. A3)

The unique identity of the Rangers was intermingled with stories of igloos, snowmobiles, and traditional knowledge. As such, the Rangers were described as "Arctic warriors" coming

> from all walks of life. In Ross River, there's a teacher, a mechanic, a fuel truck driver, a bank manager and a furnace repairman. Across the North, many mayors and MLAs are or have been Rangers.
>
> (VanderKlippe, January 23 2005: p. A3)

In the two previously-quoted articles, the unforgiving Arctic environment and the great distances covered by such patrols (600 kilometres for one, 1,800 kilometres for the other) were contrasted with the limited resources allocated to the Rangers to perform sovereignty patrols. Snowmobiles and old Lee Enfield rifles were juxtaposed to traditional Inuit knowledge and were presented as potential resources to better assert sovereignty.

Out of the 66 articles published from 2002 to 2005, more than one third (23 articles) had for primary focus of interest the coverage of the CF-led sovereignty patrols. Other than asserting sovereignty on the Canadian Arctic, these deployments increased media coverage of the region. The increase of interest in 2003 and especially 2004 was due to journalists covering these sovereignty-assertion patrols. This can be observed by focusing on the time of the year in which these articles were published, with clear peaks showing in August (operation NARWHAL was usually held in August but extended into September in 2004) and April, when a sovereignty operation involving the Canadian Rangers would typically be held (see Figure 2.2).

As a result, CF personnel and Rangers were also considered as external sources of authority by journalists, and as such were often quoted as credible sources of knowledge on the field. While representing only 30% of passages quoted in our overall sample, they constituted 50% of experts solicited in the 23 articles dealing with sovereignty exercises. At this point, it is of significant importance to figure out whether these authorities spread alarmist or reassuring assessments of CASS issues. As part of the public sector, these actors could be expected to abide by departmental lines. After all, they needed to seek approval from a superior in many cases before talking to the media. However, a rich literature studying the agent–principal relationship documented that the link between an authority (principal) and a subordinate (agent) is not so clear-cut; the agent often has room for initiative (Rauchhaus, 2009; Elsig, 2011).

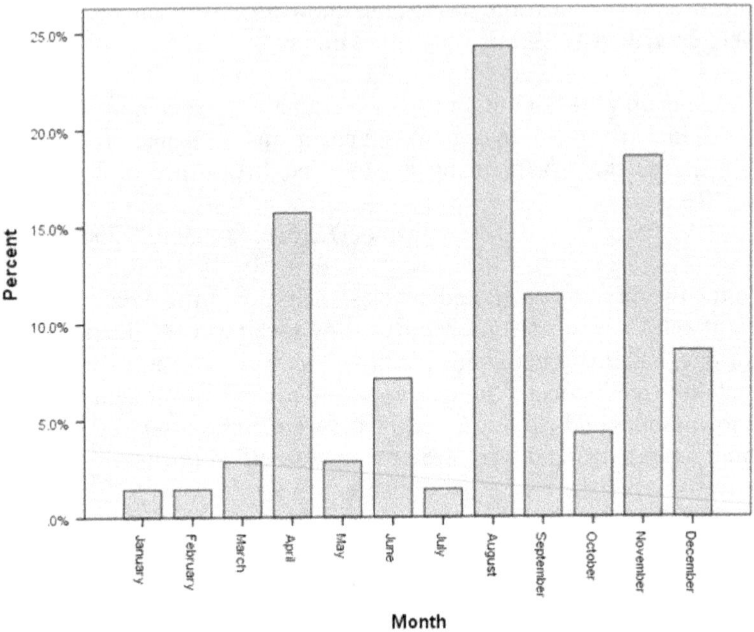

Figure 2.2 Percentage of journalistic articles published in 15 Canadian newspapers from June 2000 to April 2005 by month.

For the purpose of this book, one could argue that these agents could have expressed two different points of view. For one, CF personnel could have adopted a strategy consisting of downplaying threats to Canadian claims. This would have for main objective to comfort the Canadian population as to the status of the Canadian Arctic and to emphasize on governmental actions undertaken to assert CASS. This type of assessment framed the Canadian government as actively protecting the Canadian Arctic and being in control of the situation.

On the other hand, CF personnel could have attempted to raise public awareness on the nature of threats that Canada faced in the Arctic. This narrative could have served as an efficient way to attract people's attention, to generate support for further investments in the region and to help justify current operations.

In total, acting CF personnel or Canadian Rangers accounted for 51 interventions. For the most part, these individuals were called upon to give technical or operational details. This served the purpose of enriching the storyline with outside sources, even though this information could have been provided by journalists. Hence, these quoted passages do not uncover much about the perceptions CF personnel and Rangers had of CASS issues.

However, an analysis of CF personnel expressing alarmist or reassuring opinions on CASS issues offers inconclusive evidence. Five passages were classified as reassuring assessments downplaying the seriousness of external threats, while five others were deemed alarmist, with only two of these five mentioning the use-it-or-lose-it idea. Seven CF personnel underlined the lack of resources devoted to assert Canadian control over the Arctic and called for more resources to be invested in order to strengthen Canadian capabilities.

These observations may be contrasted with opinions expressed by public servants from other departments to evaluate if and how CF personnel perceptions differed from that of other employees from the public sector. Fifteen interventions from bureaucrats were printed. A reassuring tone was unveiled, with 6 of the 15 actually downplaying the seriousness of Arctic threats, and only one promoting an alarmist standpoint. No bureaucrats were quoted or paraphrased expressing the use-it-or-lose-it principle. So comparatively speaking, CF personnel were more prone to promote pessimistic scenarios on CASS issues than other governmental officials.

However, military personnel do not stand out when compared with the rest of the sample. As seen in Table 2.3, about an equal number of pessimistic and reassuring assessments could be accounted for once public servants and military personnel were excluded from the sample.

Looking at these observations, one may find it difficult to consider these experts as purveyors of polar peril. All in all, journalists offered a balanced perspective, able to present both the pessimistic and optimistic interpretations of Canada's future prospects in regards to what it claims to be its Arctic. Quantitatively, optimists and pessimists were interviewed in near equal numbers. However, a careful examination of the articles gathered leaves the reader with a recurring impression that the focus was definitely more pessimistic and alarmist than reassuring. Journalistic practices must be scrutinized to document this persistent perception.

Table 2.3 Distribution of types of assessments by categories of experts

	Reassuring	*Pessimistic*	*Alarmist/Use-it-or-lose-it*
CF personnel	5	5	2
Public servants	6	1	0
All other experts	25	27	8

The ways of the journalists

If not quantitative in nature, pessimistic assessments could have enjoyed a qualitative advantage, having been printed in prime spaces in these newspapers. An inconclusive outcome was reached on this front as well: very few articles on Arctic issues were published as front page story as a meagre 13% of articles compiled (9 out of 70 articles) fit this description. By widening the premium space definition to the first three pages of the first section of a newspaper (so A1–A3 or page 1–3) and the front page of subsequent sections (B1 or C1, for examples), a more substantial subsection of our sample was created, covering close to 1 out of 3 articles. Alarmist expert evaluations were as frequent as optimistic ones; alarmist assessments did not seem to sell, or at the very least, generate enough impact to justify occupying premium spots.

Positioning within the newspaper was not everything; some experts' testimonies could be put on the spotlight within the article at the detriment of other experts. On this front, there is evidence that alarmist opinions were often inserted as part of the title of numerous articles. A good illustration of this tendency can be seen in an article written by VanderKlippe again, this time published in three different newspapers (*Edmonton Journal, Ottawa Citizen,* and *Times Colonist*). The journalist reported on different opinions voiced at a Northern Research Forum workshop, an international forum bringing academics and stakeholders together to discuss matters relevant to Northern communities.

The article presented both alarmist and reassuring accounts of the Arctic security environment. The articles entitled "Arctic vulnerable to terrorists" (VanderKlippe, September 19 2004: p. A1) and "Arctic a potential terror target" (VanderKlippe, September 19 2004a: p. A3), presented a choice of framing by the reporter that was straightforward: the region was potentially threatened by dark forces. The piece described the more widespread fears about the Canadian Arctic, without much explanation as to how these different elements were connected. It opened on the following claim: "resource development sweeps across Canada's North" turning the region into one of "strategic importance." It subsequently quoted then Commander of CF Northern Area, Norm Couturier, describing the Arctic as an emerging battlefield in the war on terrorism: "As the circumpolar countries raise the profile of the Arctic… (it) then becomes a new target for international terrorism" (Couturier cited in VanderKlippe, September 19 2004: p. A1). Hence, new resources exploitation projects were associated with heightened fears of terrorism, even though the connection between the two was dubious. Called the "soft belly of the continent" against terrorist infiltrations, the Arctic was described in dark terms by VanderKlippe, a region that was already tackling organized crime, illegal immigration and contrabands. The article also concluded by quoting a worrisome security assessment: fear was now publicly expressed not by a CF commander, but by a member of a Northern community, thus highlighting that these threats also worried Northerners. Frank Pokiak, a Tuktoyaktuk local representative, spoke of the fear that terrorists might attack strategic infrastructures present in Canada's North. In his words, "If terrorists decide to invade our country, those DEW-line sites are going to be the first to be hit [...] They could wipe out the whole community" (VanderKlippe, September 19 2004: p. A1). The terminology used is striking: notions of invasion and community survival were employed. This added to the confusion about the nature of the threat; from then on, terrorists were not only connected to resources but also to military infrastructures. Nothing was mentioned about the very low symbolic and strategic importance of these radar sites, relics of the Cold War and remnants of antiquated strategic considerations.

The article also balanced this dark security evaluation with voices downplaying the seriousness of these threats. Squeezed between the fear-mongering introduction and conclusion, Rob Huebert underlined that "the military threats to the North are negligible" (Huebert cited in VanderKlippe, September 19 2004b: p. A3). Icelandic president Olafur Ragmar Grimsson was also quoted, downplaying the likelihood of terrorist attacks in the Arctic region, claiming that the risk was low and urging restraint on alarming security discourses. However, Grimsson's opinion was immediately countered by Pokiak's DEW line concern. Here, the importance of these reassuring observations was tempered with the claim that these fears had already infiltrated into people's minds: "Even so, the perception of vulnerability to terror has begun to worry some northerners" (VanderKlippe, September 19 2004a: p. A3). Perceptions were casted as more relevant than facts or objective reality.

Hence, although optimistic voices were included in the article, they did not constitute the main frame, as emphasized by the title. Further, pessimistic claims made for the bulk of the article. In the version printed in the *Ottawa Citizen*, 65% of the article (312 out of the 477 words) presented the reader with alarmist accounts. Similar observations could be made for the *Times Colonist* and *Edmonton Journal* versions of this article. In all three cases, such framing allowed a rather mundane academic conference report to make it into the first three pages of all three publications (and front page in the case of the *Edmonton Journal*).

At other times, the main story consisted of a focus on expert's assessments. Such accounts in reference to the CF could be observed in the early 2000s. David Pugliese's article, published in December 2000 and entitled "Arctic sovereignty at risk: Military warns North's riches open to plunder by foreign lands; Threat rises as Forces' power slips," presented the CF prediction on Arctic security and sovereignty. The article, published on the *Ottawa Citizen's* front page, presented in great details a report made by the CF forecasting the future of the Canadian Arctic. The list of threats mentioned was exhaustive and the consequences of inaction were dire:

> Billions of dollars worth of Canadian Arctic resources are open for plunder by other nations because of a dwindling military and government presence in the region [...] Everything from fish to fresh water could be scooped up by other countries as the Arctic is made more accessible by global warming and resources in other parts of the world decrease.
>
> (Pugliese, December 7 2000: p. A1)

This military assessment was uncontested by other experts. Indeed, all experts cited or paraphrased were from military ranks and shared the report's main conclusions; no additional expert opinions were sought by the journalist.

Overall, looking at headlines, the pessimistic frame seemed to gather more steam in journalistic practices than the reassuring one. A total of 15 titles propagated pessimistic or alarmist ideas about Canada's Arctic sovereignty and security, while no title actively downplayed threats to Canada's North. Focusing on these 15 articles, repetitions of certain themes strike the reader. First, the notion that Canadian sovereignty was at risk came back numerous times, coupled with the notion that the country was contemplating losing part to its Arctic to others. "Others may soon exploit Canada's North" (*Vancouver Sun*, March 5 2005: p. D18) and "Canada's claim on islands is weak" (Duffy, December 7 2000: p. A2) are titles illustrative of this pattern. One can also notice that at the very least, images of confrontation and battle were portrayed: the articles "Rough seas ahead – Sovereignty: Challenges will increase with global warming" (Farrell, September 18 2002: p. I10), Pugliese's "Sovereignty at risk" (Pugliese, December 7 2000: p. A1) and "A battle brews for 'our true North'" (Garvey, August 7 2004: p. A4) were all examples of this tendency.

In order to go beyond headlines, understanding the issue frames used by reporters may help further our comprehension of the phenomenon. The above-cited article by Bruce Garvey is interesting to analyze as it embodied the journalistic preferred narrative. The article was published in three publications in total (*Winnipeg Free Press, Ottawa Citizen,* and *Vancouver Sun*), and casted the Arctic as a military hot spot and a site of future (sovereignty) battle. In his piece, Garvey attempted to convey the gravity of the situation, setting the tone in the introduction by pinpointing the threat and deploying a grand arsenal of military vocabulary:

"As new technology and the melting ice cap open our northern frontier to commercial development and navigation, Canada must figure out how to assert its sovereignty against the United States. Two weeks from now Canada's depleted and far-flung military diverts its attention from hot spots such as Afghanistan, the Balkans, and Haiti, to invade the Arctic. [...] Behind it lies the ominous fact that a no-holds-barred diplomatic war is about to break out over Canada's claimed sovereignty of the islands and waters of the Arctic archipelago. And it's a war we could lose" (Garvey, August 7 2004: p. A4).

Asserting the United States as the primary threat, Garvey positioned the Arctic alongside conflict-ridden countries deemed as regions the Canadian military "invades." This invasion analogy set the reader to accept the idea that a "no-holds-barred diplomatic war" was a certainty in the near future. Note that the term "diplomatic" was dropped in the following sentence, leaving the reader with only the term "war." Here, the reporter continued with a fallacy, embracing the use-it or-lose-it idea and declaring that Canada's sovereignty over the whole Arctic (including the uncontested archipelago) was threatened.

Consequently, the situation was set by the journalist himself: Canada was at war with the world's superpower for the possession of the whole Arctic, with only a "depleted and far-flung military" to count on. Garvey then turned his attention to explaining how this came to be. His historical review could have begun with the first Canada–US frictions in the 1950s centring continental defence, or the 1969 Manhattan transit (since the US are the enemy...). However, he instead went further back in history connecting the explorers of the past which defied the harsh Arctic environment with federal policies:

> Scattered as it is with the lure of names such as Hudson, Frobisher and Franklin, the Arctic exerts an almost magical hold on Canadian emotions, despite long periods of neglect interspersed with intense expressions of our attachment.
>
> (Garvey, August 7 2004: p. A4)

This era, linked to emotions and expressions of nostalgic nationalism, though contrasted with the pragmatic present, was one in which strategic, geopolitical, and interest-driven considerations had to dominate;

> Today it's no romantic Diefenbaker-like vision that's driving the international debate over who owns the Arctic ice islands and waterways. Advances in technology and global warming promise to diminish the polar icecap and open the frontier to increasing commercial development and navigation. A trove of oil, diamonds, fresh water, fish stocks and minerals awaits. A navigable Northwest Passage could replace the Panama Canal as the prime East-West trade route.
>
> (Garvey, August 7 2004: p. A4)

A review of failed attempts by the federal government to better control and ensure adequate surveillance of the region was detailed. The article concluded on assessing the impact of Inuit occupation of the Arctic in order to assert Canada's claims. While it was stated that the Inuit accounted for "much of Canada's claim to the North," the Inuit were also presented as ill-equipped to face these threats:

> Militarily, however, the operation of the Canadian Rangers in a high-tech world of satellite surveillance and nuclear submarines is little more than useless. The recruited Inuit, carrying ancient 303 rifles and wearing Ranger baseball caps, combine regular hunting trips with official patrols, keeping an outdoorsman's keen eye open for any foreign or suspicious presence among the ice flows.
>
> (Garvey, August 7 2004: p. A4)

This type of narrative was not bound to one article; it was found in multiple journalistic articles dealing with Canada's Arctic sovereignty and security from 2000 to 2005. In other pieces, the early 20th century exploration movement was compared to a renewed "worldwide competition" to come (Duffy, December 7 2000: p. A2), while reporter Jim Farrell noted that "after a 70-year lull, the centuries-old battle for Arctic sovereignty may heat up again" (Farrell, September 18 2002: p. I10). The battle and competition images have remained to this day popular predictions among journalists.

Setting the stage… for a barren rock

Reviewing journalistic articles highlights the great importance that experts play in describing current events and providing analytical insights.

They are quoted or paraphrased to propel the story line, express points of views that the journalistic ethic of objectivity forbids journalists to partake in or offer background to stories. Experts opinions were sought in every article reviewed.

When analyzed as a group, pessimistic predicaments from experts were not found to be dominant from 2000 to 2005. Experts voicing optimistic and pessimistic frames about Canada's Arctic sovereignty and security were found in almost equal numbers. As such it would appear that journalists made an effort to offer a balanced perspective to their readership by presenting both sides of any given issue. However, other than the experts interviewed, these same journalists made great use of the pessimistic and, from time to time, alarmist frames when describing the changing Arctic geopolitical context in the first half of the 2000s. Global warming was framed as unleashing dark forces threatening the country's sovereignty and security, challenges for which Canada was described as being ill-equipped to confront. Journalists, in numerous news articles, clearly preferred the alarmist frame in order to develop rich narratives and hook their readers.

Of course, with hindsight, one can point at the absurdity of warning against terrorist infiltrations in the Arctic region: no expert would even raise the idea in public today, lest to make their audience laugh. This highlights how Arctic security discourses cannot be dissociated from broader security frames (e.g., the war on terrorism), and that attempting to attract attention to the Arctic region in this manner can be rather misleading and counter-productive.

Consequences of this bias on public opinion and governments are difficult to assess. Of course, one cannot earnestly claim that media reports account for the shift in Canadian Arctic policy as stated in the 2005 Canada's international statement *Pride and Influence in the World*; this would be rather simplistic and unsubstantiated. However, repetitions of the same idea can strengthen social acceptability and contribute to turning specific interpretations of reality into uncontested fact; further, it plays on perceptions of the nature of the Arctic region, and what it will be confronted to in the near or distant future. This sets up a context in which events supporting this interpretation could be blown out of proportion and instrumentalized by media and governments alike. Agenda setting then becomes possible when an event fits the preferred frame.

The best example of such an event came at the end of July 2005. Hans Island is a tiny rock set perfectly at the midpoint between Ellesmere Island on the Canadian side and Greenland on the Danish side in the High Arctic Nares strait. The island is a barren one, harbouring neither population nor resource. It is, however, a contested territory as neither country ever signed an agreement pertaining to the ownership of the island. Both countries had been sending expeditions to Hans Island since the 1980s to assert their claims over the territory. Denmark sent an expedition to the island in 2002 and 2003, planting the Danish flag on its surface. The Government of Canada decided in the summer of 2004 to do the same, sending CF on 13 July 2005 to affirm Canadian sovereignty over the island. On 20 July 2005, then Defence minister Bill Graham flew to Hans Island with CF personnel to plant a Canadian flag and build several inuksuit.

Graham's visit spurred a minor diplomatic spat with Denmark, who issued a diplomatic note of protest. Discussions ensued between both parties in early August to resolve the matter diplomatically, with an outcome reached on 19 September 2005. Low-level bureaucratic exchanges have been the preferred way to deal with this matter, for which no permanent resolution has been reached as of 2019. Hence, this in no way equates to a major conflict with great stakes at hand.

However, it would be rather difficult to reach such a conclusion if one exclusively looked at the overwhelming media attention this event generated. In the two weeks following Graham's visit, 43 journalistic articles were published in the same sample of newspapers previously studied in this chapter, which consisted of more than 60% of the articles written from June 2000 to April 2005. To these 43 articles were added 35 editorials printed from 20 July 2005 to the 19 September 2005 (Landriault, 2013: p. 131).

Seen as a precedent for the battle and competition to come, the profile of the Hans Island dispute was heightened to the point of framing the ownership of the barren rock as a test of Canada's sovereignty, one that if lost could lead to a domino effect engulfing the entire Canadian Arctic. The domino logic was also reinforced by means of public declarations made by the acting government. Bill Graham addressed the issue of the status of the NWP on 31 July during an interview with CTV's Question Period in which he stated that:

> We actually have a dispute with the United States [...] and our view is that's the internal waters of Canada given the layout of the Continental Shelf and our historic exercise of sovereignty over that area.
> (Blanchfield, August 1 2005: p. A10)

While still a rather benign statement in nature, segments of the interview became the subject of nine articles, printed by publications from coast to coast. The headlines[5] used strong wording to frame the minister's thoughts. Graham's comments were quite timely as well: with a general election right around the corner, and a Liberal government depicting the Leader of the Opposition, Stephen Harper, as being too close to the Americans, mentioning the Canada–US dispute on the status of the NWP was clearly not random.

The construction of threats observed from 2000 to 2005 may explain why the Hans island dispute was considered so paramount: the idea of upcoming dangers was reinforced time and again in the media. It was also the prelude of a more activist period in Canada's Arctic policy, one that was to see intense political messaging carried out by government in order to define and ultimately shape the Canadian Arctic.

Notes

1 Those newspapers are: *Calgary Herald, Edmonton Journal, Globe and Mail, Kingston Whig-Standard, Leader Post, Montreal Gazette, National Post, Ottawa Citizen, Star Phoenix, Sudbury Star, The Province, Times Colonist, Toronto Star, Vancouver Sun,* and *Winnipeg Free Press.*

2 Griffiths and Lackenbauer often voiced that some academics were spreading alarmist accounts of Canadian Arctic sovereignty. Although Griffiths and Lackenbauer never provided specific names, Rob Huebert immediately comes to mind given that he has warned of impending dangers about to hit Canada's Arctic policy, describing these forces as combining in a perfect storm (Huebert, 2009).

3 Canadian Forces personnel, Rangers and members of the US military were included in the military personnel category.

4 Elected representatives at the federal, provincial, or municipal levels were considered as political representatives.

5 Such headlines included: "Canada to U.S.: Passage is ours: Heated warming following spat with Danes", "Hands off Northwest Passage, Graham tells Washington" or "Northwest Passage is Canadian territory, Graham warns U.S."

References

Appelbe, Alison. August 27 2002. Canada Revives Claim of Arctic Sovereignty. *Montreal Gazette*, p. A16.

Blanchfield, Mike. August 1 2005. Lay Off Northwest Passage, Defence Minister Tells U.S. *Montreal Gazette*, p. A10.

Chater, Andrew. 2012. Beyond the "Golly-Gee" Stage. *International Journal*, volume 67, issue 3: pp. 831–47.

Department of Foreign Affairs and International Trade of Canada. 2000. *The Northern Dimension of Canada's Foreign Policy* (last checked September 27 2016) http://gac.canadiana.ca/view/ooe.b3651149E/1?r=0&s=1

Department of National Defence of Canada. 2005. *A Role of Pride and Influence in the World – Defence* (last checked August 31 2016) http://publications.gc.ca/site/eng/9.687487/publication.html

Duffy, Andrew. December 7 2000. Canada's Claim on Islands Is Weak, Arctic Expert Warns. *Ottawa Citizen*, p. A2.

Elsig, Manfred. 2011. Principal-Agent Theory and the World Trade Organization: Complex Agency and "Missing Delegation". *European Journal of International Relations*, volume 17, issue 3: pp. 495–517.

Farrell, Jim. Sovereignty: Challenges Will Increase with Global Warming. *Edmonton Journal*, September 18 2002, p. I10.

Garvey, Bruce. August 7 2004. A Battle Brews for "Our True North". *Ottawa Citizen*, p. A4.

Griffiths, Franklyn. 2003. The Shipping News: Canada's Arctic Sovereignty Not on Thinning Ice. *International Journal*, volume 58, issue 2: pp. 257–82.

Huebert, Rob. 2009. Canada and the Changing International Arctic: At the Crossroads of Cooperation and Conflict. In Frances Abele, Thomas J. Courchene, F. Leslie Seidle and France St-Hilaire (eds.) *Northern Exposure: Peoples, Powers and Prospects for Canada's North*. Institute for Research on Public Policy, Montreal: pp. 77–106.

Huebert, Rob. 2003. The Shipping News Part II – How Canada's Arctic Sovereignty Is on Thinning Ice. *International Journal*, volume 58, issue 3: pp. 295–308.

Landriault, Mathieu. 2013. La sécurité arctique 2000–2010: une décennie turbulente? Ph.D. Dissertation, University of Ottawa (last checked February 6 2017) www.ruor.uottawa.ca/handle/10393/24353

Pugliese, David. December 7 2000. Arctic Sovereignty at Risk: Military Warns North's Riches Open to Plunder by Foreign Lands. *Ottawa Citizen*, p. A1.

Rauchhaus, Robert. 2009. Principal-agent Problems in Humanitarian Intervention: Moral Hazards, Adverse Selection, and the Commitment Dilemma. *International Studies Quarterly*, volume 53, issue 4: pp. 871–84.

Rempel, Shauna. September 22, 2003. Climate Change Tops Agenda at Arctic Sovereignty Conference. *Star-Phoenix*, p. A4.

Roussel, Stéphane. 2010. Continentalisme et nouveau discours sécuritaire: le Grand Nord assiégé. In F. Lasserre (ed.) Passages et mers arctiques – Géopolitique d'une région en mutation. Presses de l'Université du Québec, Québec: pp. 161–84.

Struzik, Ed. November 5 2000. Melting Polar Ice Poses New Challenges to Canada's Control Over the Fabled Northwest Passage. *Edmonton Journal*, p. E7.

Toronto Star. June 9 2000. Arctic Set for a $10 Million Windfall; Canada Must Assert Interests in North: Axworthy, p. A6.

Vancouver Sun. March 5 2005. Others May Soon Exploit Canada's North, an Author Warns, p. D18.

VanderKlippe, Nathan. January 23 2005. Arctic Warriors North: Mid-winter Patrols Hone Military and Traditional Skills. *Edmonton Journal*, p. A3.

VanderKlippe, Nathan. September 19 2004a. Arctic a Potential Terror Target. *Ottawa Citizen*, p. A3.

VanderKlippe, Nathan. September 19 2004b. Arctic Could Be Target for Terrorism. *Times Colonist*, p. A3.

VanderKlippe, Nathan. September 19 2004. Arctic a Potential Terror Target. *Edmonton Journal*, p. A1.

VanderKlippe, Nathan. April 17 2004. Trek Enforces Sovereignty on “the Edge”. *Edmonton Journal*, p. A17.

3 Touring a (melting) ice pack

Canada's Arctic sovereignty and security policy experienced a renaissance in the early 2000s. With global warming around the corner, the Government of Canada under Jean Chrétien and Paul Martin shied away from the liberal internationalist perspective put on paper in the 2000 *Northern Dimension* policy statement (see Chapter 2). The focus turned instead to the necessity to re-invest in surveillance capabilities and beef up sovereignty patrols and military assets to patrol the region. To be fair, parts of the approach detailed in the 2000 policy document are still present in the 2005 foreign policy statement, *A Role of Pride and Influence in the World*, though in a lesser prominent position. The commerce section of the 2005 document referred to the region once, stressing that "cooperation with Russian Arctic economic development is a priority area of mutual benefit," highlighting the potential of emerging markets for "Canadian–Russian joint ventures exploiting Siberia's vast natural resources" (Department of Foreign Affairs and International Trade, 2005a: p. 21).

In the diplomacy section, the Arctic was inserted as a component in the North American partnership sub-section. The country was deemed able to assume a "leadership role in the circumpolar world," in alignment with the 2000 orientation. Declined in a single paragraph, the list of initiatives needed to take on such an important role was quite thin: cooperation at the Arctic Council on climate change adaptation and promotion of the 2007/2008 International Polar year were the only two concrete initiatives detailed within the paragraph (Department of Foreign Affairs and International Trade, 2005b: p. 8). The proactive, bold language of 2000 had disappeared, leaving the country with a rather passive and reactive diplomatic stance towards the region.

The bulk of new initiatives was located in the defence section of the 2005 statement. One of the five key priorities in regards to national security enunciated in the defence section of the document was that the Canadian Forces (CF) should "increase their efforts to ensure the sovereignty and security of our territory, airspace and maritime approaches, including in the Arctic" (Department of National Defence, 2005: p. 17).

The Arctic was also implicitly connected to other priorities such as improving the use of information gathered and expanding Forces' presence and mobility across Canada. Naturally, enhanced Northern capabilities were promised to meet these new challenges. Improving the Canadian Rangers' ability, modernizing Aurora long-range maritime patrol aircrafts, replacing the Twin Otter fleet and harnessing the potential of satellites and radars were examples of such increased levels of commitment (Department of National Defence, 2005: pp. 18–20).

Sovereignty affirmation patrols and responsiveness exercises predate the 2005 policy document. The annual NARWHAL operation was functional from 2002 to 2007, at which point it was replaced by both operations NUNALIVUT (smaller, typically every April) and NANOOK (larger deployment, typically every August). Sovereignty patrols were also conducted to complete operation NARWHAL. For example, operations BEAUFORT and LANCASTER exemplified such maneuvers in 2006, ensuring surveillance in the Western and Eastern Canadian Arctic, respectively.

NARWHAL, in 2002 and from 2004 to 2006, as well as NANOOK from 2007 onwards represented the biggest deployments: hundreds of participants and 10+ different stakeholders were involved, from federal departments to private companies and municipal and territorial agencies. These were designed as exercises to train CF alongside other governmental agencies facing diverse challenges that could potentially erupt in the Canadian Arctic. Training scenarios were illustrative of the nature of the challenges perceived by the governmental machinery: they resembled threats raised by experts defending a pessimistic view of Arctic security and sovereignty issues (see Chapter 2). Table 3.1 lists the training scenarios for these deployments, from 2004 to 2011.

CF personnel were trained primarily to coordinate actions against public safety threats, and mostly against non-state actors/dangers. In most cases, if any of these scenarios were to materialize elsewhere in Canada, the RCMP or Coast Guard would be the lead agency in law enforcement operations. It is worth noting that CF do not undertake the tasks traditionally expected of them. In fact, military personnel in the Arctic are called upon to ensure environmental protection, to engage in search-and-rescue operations, to prevent illegal trafficking, and to manage public health crisis. Out of these 15 scenarios, only one may be labelled a traditional defence concern: anti-submarine warfare. These exercises highlight the unusual function undertaken by the CF in the Canadian Arctic. As seen in Chapter 2, these deployments

Table 3.1 Scenarios simulated in NARWHAL and NANOOK sovereignty operations from 2004 to 2011

Year	*Scenario 1*	*Scenario 2*	*Scenario 3*
NARHWAL 2004	Foreign satellite crashing		
NARWHAL 2005	Threats to oil and gas industry	Search-and-rescue for major airline disaster	
NARWHAL 2006	Terrorist threats to the energy sector	Public health emergency	Crash of a commercial passenger aircraft
NANOOK 2007	Oil spill	drug smuggling	
NANOOK 2008	Ship in distress – Disease outbreak	Oil spill	
NANOOK 2009	Anti-submarine warfare	Downed drone	Threat to critical infrastructure on land
NANOOK 2010	Petrochemical spill on land		
NANOOK 2011	Air-disaster/ search-and-rescue operation		

Source: National Defence of Canada.

increased the amount of media coverage on Arctic issues. They act as singular events leading to talks about security and sovereignty issues. Their profile was only heightened with the elections of the first minority Conservative government in January 2006.

Use it or lose it: A Conservative Arctic policy

The Conservative Party of Canada was elected by the Canadian people to form government following the 2006 general elections, after a 13-year hiatus from power. This electoral campaign was unusually long, beginning on 29 November, with the election day scheduled for 23 January 2006. The Arctic made a surprise (although brief) appearance as a topic in the 2005–2006 federal elections campaign. On 19 December 2005, the *National Post* revealed that a US submarine, the USS Charlotte, which had started its course on the American West coast, had reached the North Pole on 10 November, before surfacing by breaking through ice. It had then rallied the US East coast, presumably[1] by going through Canadian waters in the Nares and Davis straits.

This scoop was revealed following frictions between the incumbent Prime Minister Paul Martin and the American administration. In early December, Martin publicly criticized the US for their inaction on the climate change file, following the United Nations Conference on Climate Change held in Montreal. The Prime Minister went on to say that "there are nations that resist, voices that attempt to diminish the urgency," pointing fingers in the direction of the Americans at a subsequent news conference: "To the reticent nations, including the United States, I say there is such a thing as a global conscience, and now is the time to listen to it" (Cited in Gorrie and Calamai, December 8 2005: p. A6).

The US ambassador to Canada, David Wilkins, replied to Martin's plea by asking party leaders to restrain themselves. Wilkins remarked that "All of us should hope it does not have a long-term impact on our relationship. And that is what you have to weigh scoring short-term political points against," adding that "Canada never has to tear the U.S. down to build itself up" (Cited in Delacourt and Mills, December 14 2005: p. A8). Hence, the news release of the USS Charlotte transit happened in a time of Canada–US friction. The timing of the revelation was rather odd, as it made headlines five days after Wilkins's intervention. This oddity was highlighted by the fact that the transit was carried out in November, reaching its final destination on the US East Coast at the end of the said month. Thus, the USS Charlotte had already arrived at destination when the scandal broke out. This consequently put the Liberals in defensive mode, as they scrambled to come up with a coherent response to explain the incident. The Liberals were at pain to give further information on the transit, hinting indirectly that they were unaware if such transit had even occurred or not (Landriault, 2013: p. 166).

The Conservatives jumped on this opportunity, deploying in full display the pessimistic assessment described in Chapter 2. Alarmism was front and centre, mixing territorial integrity and natural resources. In the words of then Conservative defence critic Gordon O'Connor, "Our sovereignty is being challenged and will continue to be challenged as other nations covet our vast resources" (Cited in Wattie and Weeks, December 20 2005: p. A9). Stephen Harper went even further, brandishing the possibility of losing territory if inactive:

> We would hope that an aggressive approach to our sovereignty would persuade countries to respect that sovereignty and to obviously deal with us before they send vessels in our water [...] sovereignty is something that you use it or you lose it.
>
> (Cited in Gordon, December 23 2005: p. A6)

Harpers' Conservatives quickly changed their game plan, preceding an Arctic announcement scheduled for later during the campaign. On December 22, Stephen Harper unveiled the Conservative plan to strengthen Arctic sovereignty and security. The plan included purchasing three armed icebreakers, building a deep-water docking facility and stationing 500 troops in Iqaluit as well as implementing an underwater system to detect submarine activity. This last measure addressed the USS Charlotte incident directly, emphasizing on the need to know who was under the ice pack. The main objective of the Conservative plan was to boost Canadian capabilities in the Arctic region by putting "boots on the tundra" and providing key military assets to the CF in order to ensure surveillance of the region. The price tag that was provided was a rough estimate, totalling two billion dollars over eight or nine years (Landriault, 2013: p. 168).

Attention for the Arctic subsided following the Conservative announcement, the holiday break helping change the focus of the electoral campaign. The region came back on the political agenda only after the election of the Conservatives to form government. At the end of his first press conference, Prime Minister designate Stephen Harper responded to comments made the day before by US ambassador Wilkins in a talk given at Western University. In his talk, Wilkins reiterated the long-standing American position that the American government did not recognize Canadian sovereignty over the Northwest Passage (NWP). Harper went unprompted by journalists on the matter and objected:

> The Canadian government will defend our sovereignty. I've been very clear in the campaign that we have significant plans for National Defence and for defence of our sovereignty including Arctic sovereignty. We believe we have a mandate for those from the Canadian people and we hope to have it as well from the House of Commons but it is the Canadian people we get our mandate from, not the Ambassador of the United States.
>
> (Canadian Press, January 26 2006)

However, the first few months of the first Harper minority government were uneventful on the Arctic front. No major announcement was made and no new development to fulfil the Conservative electoral promise was observed. The reality of power started to establish itself, with some components of the electoral promise bearing the potential to spark a radical overhaul of Canada's Arctic policy. As pointed out by Franklyn Griffiths, the underwater detection system had the potential to hinder the Canada–US bilateral relationship:

> for the Prime Minister to persist in a mistaken naval defence of Arctic sovereignty would be worse than counterproductive for Canada–U.S. relations. Consider first what might happen when new naval icebreakers and sensors are in place. A submarine is detected and the acoustic signature tells us whose it is. It's American. What then do we do? Have troops lean over the icebreaker rail and shake their fists at the sub as it passes by under the ice? Launch depth charges from an icebreaker onto a nuclear-powered submarine? To avert any such insanity (and to save billions of dollars), the Prime Minister ought to cancel the naval icebreaker commitment.
>
> (Griffiths, February 22 2006: p. A21)

Promised military acquisitions were reconsidered and downsized in terms of both number and capability. The three icebreakers were downsized to one icebreaker (without the armed component) as six to eight offshore patrols ships (capable of cutting through merely one meter of ice) were preferred by the Government of Canada. These investments were announced at a later time in the summers of 2007 (for the offshore patrol ships) and 2008 (for the icebreaker).

The Canadian Arctic was considered important by the Harper government in other ways. In fact, the annual Prime Ministerial tours, starting in the summer of 2006, quickly became a staple of the Harper years.

Prime Ministerial annual Arctic tours

The importance of the region was rendered evident by the level of attention devoted to the Arctic by the Prime Minister. Even though Prime Minister Martin visited the region in 2004, the profile of these visits was heightened under Prime Minister Harper. These annual tours focused on the North in a more general manner as the Prime Minister visited all three Northern territories: Nunavut, the Northwest Territories and Yukon. Of the three, Nunavut was evidently the one most intimately tied to Arctic sovereignty and security issues. The relevance of the Northwest Territories for Arctic issues was reflected by the presence of the headquarters of the CF Joint Task Force North based in Yellowknife. These tours also extended to Manitoba (in Churchill) and Northern Quebec (Nunavik); however, these stops were exceptions rather than the norm.

The geographical remoteness of the region also made it so that the media would have to send national affairs reporters to cover the tours. This dynamic made control over the media easier to achieve for the Prime Minister's Office (PMO), given that journalists followed the schedule and the official activities of the Prime Minister. This control was highly criticized by journalists due to both the ambiguity surrounding the notion of who was allowed to ask questions, and to tight monitoring of the time actually allocated to the journalists' questions. In the words of a reporter who followed the PM tour for Radio-Canada:

> The control exercised by the Prime Minister's Office is regularly denounced by the media. At every press conference, they limit the number of questions. The reporters determine the topics and who will speak. Today, six names were submitted but the office of Stephen Harper limited the number of questions to five.
>
> (*Le Téléjournal*, August 23 2013)

Political messaging was then facilitated to promote announcements and to conduct photo operations that presented Stephen Harper under a favourable light to the Canadian people. Above all, it highlighted the importance this government bestowed to the Arctic file. On this regard, the first tour was indicative of the trade-off favoured by the government as well as demonstrative of the importance of the Arctic for this new government. An international conference on AIDS was held in Toronto from 13 to 18 August. The Prime Minister had decided to undertake his first Arctic tour during this period, going North from 11 to 17 August. Harper's "no show" at the AIDS conference brought forth a storm of criticisms, from commentators, scientists and diplomats alike, calling the "no show" a mistake. Public opinion seemed to think likewise: a majority of Canadians (54%) interviewed on the matter thought the PM was wrong for not attending the international AIDS conference, with only 43% supporting the PM's decision (Ipsos Reid, 2006). Unapologetic, the Tories defended the choice of not announcing any new measures to address the AIDS issue by calling the issue "too politicized" for the moment (O'Neill and Cobb, August 18 2006: p. A11).

Beyond the controversy of the first tour, these events served as opportunities to describe the Arctic region with specific terms and to articulate the Conservative vision of the past, present, and future of the region. Harpers' tours of 2006 and 2007 were informative on this regard, explicitly demonstrating the urgency to engage in the region by imposing the use it or lose it concept.

The 2007 tour was particularly revealing on this front; it sketched a common vision of the North, one mixing nationalism and breath-taking sceneries. Hence, the North was:

> a place so stunningly beautiful that no Canadian can experience it without feeling an overwhelming sense of "romantic patriotism" for our country. Even Canadians who have never been north of 60 feel it.
> (Harper, August 10 2007)

National pride justified the need for stronger policies to defend the Canadian Arctic, especially when it was coupled with such economic potential:

> That's why we react so strongly when other countries show disrespect for our sovereignty over the Arctic [...] Canada's New Government understands the first principle of Arctic sovereignty: use it or lose it. We recognize the North is a vast storehouse of energy and mineral resources. We know that climate change is increasing accessibility to its treasures. And we understand the challenges our sovereignty in the Arctic may face.
> (Harper, August 10 2007)

Many aspects of these tours were conscious decisions taken by the Prime Minister and his entourage. The most important element was related to their timing during the year and the summer. These tours were planned to be held at the same time as the large-scale annual military exercise (operation LANCASTER in 2006 and then NANOOK) performed by the CF, usually in August or early September (see Table 3.2).

Table 3.2 Dates of both the annual Prime Ministerial tours and military exercises from 2006 to 2014

Year	*Dates of Prime Minister tours*	*Dates of military exercises*
2006	11–17 August	12–24 August
2007	7–10 August	7–17 August
2008	26–28 August	16–26 August
2009	17–21 August	6–28 August
2010	22–27 August	6–26 August
2011	23–26 August	4 August–1 September
2012	20–24 August	1–26 August
2013	18–23 August	2–23 August
2014	20–25 August	20–29 August

Note: The 2015 tour is excluded as it was part of the electoral campaign underway at that time.

The PM proceeded three times (2006, 2007, and 2014) in launching the military exercise. Harper also made it a tradition of addressing the CF partaking in operation NANOOK. Furthermore, the military exercise had been used numerous times as backdrop for various photo operations. For example, Harper was photographed in action onboard a Cormorant helicopter, while driving an all-terrain vehicle, or practicing at the shooting range with Canadian Rangers. This helped infuse the Prime Minister's tour with a definite military flavour, playing on popular perceptions that the PM visit had a heavy military focus.

However, announcements publicized during these tours were not focused solely on military initiatives. Many announcements on Arctic (and more generally Northern[2]) issues were made or repeated during these tours. Investments as well as new programmes or measures were made part of the daily press releases of the PMO or Harper's press conferences. In many instances, Harper was flanked by other members of Cabinet who had made the trip North with him. These investments were of a different nature, contrary to the persistent perception that the Conservative Arctic policy had a heavy military emphasis (see Table 3.3 for details).

Hence, varied announcements (mostly of an economic or environmental nature) were mixed in with activities of a military nature, so that military initiatives would not appear to dominate governmental political messaging. This strategy was quite politically rewarding. In fact, voter intentions for the Conservative Party of Canada went up 2.1% on average from 2006 to 2014 following these PM tours (Landriault and Minard, 2015: p. 52).

Other variables influenced the nature of the tours as well as their media exposure. For one, Russian initiatives in the Arctic were instrumentalized by the Harper government. Images of the Russian flag being deposited under the North Pole on 1 August 2007 coloured the Prime Minister's rhetoric during his tour (held the week following the event). The interception of Russian fighter jets near Canada's air space in the North in August 2008, during the PM's Arctic visit, also attracted attention. These interceptions happened days after Russia's intervention in Georgia, which generated international criticisms. These events typically increased public attention on PM visits.

The time of year in which these tours occurred was usually a slow-news period, thus facilitating greater media exposure. However, a number of unforeseen events were also put under the spotlight and monopolized people's minds: the US Presidential race (2008), the combat in Libya (2011), and the chemical attacks by the Syrian regime (2013) may very well be classified as events that eclipsed the PM tour. The PM was

Table 3.3 List of key announcements made during the Prime Minister's annual Arctic tours from 2006 to 2014

Year	*Nature of the investment/measure*	*Nature of the investment/measure*	*Nature of the investment/measure*	
2007	Environmental (Nahanni National Park)	Military (expansion of CF facilities)		
2008	Economic (Geo-mapping natural resources)	Legal (expansion of Arctic Waters Pollution Prevention Act)	Military (expansion of the Rangers program)	
2009	Economic (funding for skill training programme)	Economic (small craft harbour in Pangnirtung)	Economic (funding for highway improvements)	
2010	Scientific (High Arctic Research Station)	Scientific (support for next generation of satellites)	Environmental (Arctic marine wilderness protected area)	Social (Affordable housing)
2011	Economic (office of Chamber of Mines)	Social (Healthcare funding)	Economic (Construction of visitor centre at Kluane National Park)	
2012	Environmental (Establishment of Naats'ihch'oh National Park)	Scientific (funding for search of Franklin's lost ships)	Scientific (Funding of High Arctic Research Station)	
2013	Economic (support for mining innovation)	Economic (skills training in North)	Economic (additional resources for geo-mapping)	Environmental (clean energy project)
2014	Environmental (National Research Council's new Arctic programme)			

also compelled to address these issues or react to them, diverting attention from the daily announcements or activities scheduled.

Specific events related to domestic politics also carried a similar impact. The Maher Arar case (2007), the arrest of the Toronto 18 (2010), and Jack Layton's funeral (2011) are but a few examples of this. Other events could actually draw attention on these tours: for example, speculations on a possible federal election monopolized attention in August 2008, leading journalists to concentrate on the Arctic tour to better detect signs that the PM would soon call new elections. The minority nature of the Conservative government and the difficulty to pass the government's agenda was responsible for this heightened level of speculation.

A televised stroll

One could argue that these Arctic tours were almost designed for television, with the gorgeous Arctic landscape as natural background for announcements and events featuring the PM. Unfortunately, visual archives of news broadcasts are seldom made available, making the analysis of such an extended timeline (2006–2014) arduous. Fortunately, transcripts of such shows are made available through the database Eureka. Three news broadcasts were selected as focal points for this investigation: Radio Canada's *Le Téléjournal*, CBC's *The National* and CTV's *CTV News*. All three are national in scope, and the sample represents both public and private broadcasters, as well as both official languages.

Overall, 89 televised reports were produced during these trips from 2006 to 2014. When looking at media attention over time, one possible pattern would be that media coverage declined for these tours as time went by. The novelty effect would explain this possibility as the first few tours would draw more attention; the repetition of similar events would then generate lassitude. The period from 2006 to 2009 also brought increased activism by Arctic players, especially after the drop of the Russian flag at the bottom of the Arctic Ocean floor in the summer of 2007. The adoption of a more balanced Arctic policy and rhetoric by the Canadian government in 2009 (as illustrated in the publication of Northern Strategy policy document) put both the crisis mentality and the alarmist sovereignty discourse on the back-burner. However, media coverage generally increased during the 2006–2014 time period, 2009, 2010, and 2012 representing its peak years (see Figure 3.1).

If the number of reports had increased, the annual average length of every report did not follow the same pattern. Length may seem like a benign indicator, but it is revealing of the type of media attention devoted to Arctic issues. Indeed, the two years with the highest annual averages, 2008 (494 words) and 2009 (393 words) were the only ones during which in-depth reports were broadcasted, with two such reports being in 2008 and one being in 2009. This type of reporting provided viewers with analysis and expert opinions. In all three broadcasts, important debates and dilemma were presented: the sovereignty-on-thinning-ice debate (see Chapter 1), the challenges of

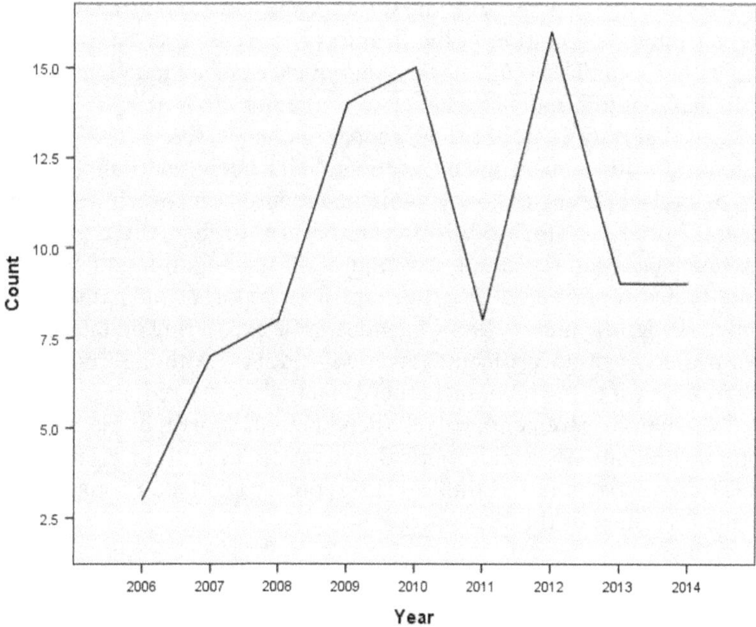

Figure 3.1 Number of televised reports in three national Canadian news broadcasts about the PM Arctic tours from 2006 to 2014.

ensuring surveillance over this vast Arctic space, or the types of solutions required to strengthen Canadian Arctic security and sovereignty were all recurrent themes. Two of these broadcasts were aired on the same day (27 August 2008) on Radio-Canada and CBC. The main frame used by reporter Frédéric Arnould on Radio-Canada had more to do with domestic politics than the Arctic itself:

> Stephen Harper en a fait son cheval de bataille. Visites répétées dans le Nord, annonces politiques et déversement de fonds de la part de ses ministres. Pas de doute, la carte du Nord est, selon Stephen Harper, devenue un de ses atouts majeurs pour une imminente campagne électorale.
>
> (*Le Téléjournal*, August 28 2008)

Here, the opportunistic nature of the Conservative plan was highlighted, with a focus on an electoralist perspective rather than the coverage of Arctic issues. For his part, CBC reporter Sasa Petricic adopted a different approach, presenting the main challenges to Canadian Arctic sovereignty. The disputes over the status of the NWP, Hans Island, and the maritime delimitation in the Beaufort Sea were described to viewers, with an emphasis put on the consequences of climate change on Canadian control and surveillance of the region. However, it must be stressed that only 3 out of the 89[3] reports gathered were of this nature, thus constituting a marginal proportion of all media attention.

The overwhelming majority of airtime focused on covering governmental initiatives albeit of a different nature. In fact, three areas of interest have been repeatedly covered: first, the beginning of the PM trips typically attracted coverage. In these reports, journalists presented the government's Arctic agenda, while expanding on intentions and evolution of governmental Arctic initiatives. Although not delving in depth into Arctic issues, they nonetheless offered an overview of Canadian involvement (or lack thereof) in its North, or framed the tour in broader domestic political dynamics, usually in relation to the electoral cycle. For example, CTV reporter Danielle Hamamdjian framed the start of the 2012 tour:

> This is trip number seven to the Arctic for Stephen Harper. Every summer he heads north for what are usually expensive, well-choreographed photo-ops. These trips are meant to promote, among other things, social development in northern communities. Part of his strategy has also been to push economic and military activity, all in the name of Arctic sovereignty, Harper's signature project. Now during the next four days he will be reminding people of previous commitments he's made. Some are on track, others are not. Far from it.
>
> (*CTV News*, August 20 2012)

Furthermore, a summary of the activities scheduled during these tours was usually presented. In the later years, the upcoming tour was also compared to past tours, in order to either underline continuity or change.

The second area of interest centred on the operational challenges and relevance of the NANOOK military deployments. Prime Minister Harper's visits at the inauguration or closing of these operations were the main reason to cover these exercises. As described by reporter Emmanuelle Latraverse,

> C'est ce qu'on appelle une démonstration de force: Stephen Harper à bord d'une frégate, entouré de sous-marins, même les avions de

> chasse sont de la partie. Une scène minutieusement orchestrée pour lancer un message sans equivoque.
>
> (*Le Téléjournal*, August 19 2009)

Covering these operations also meant having to explain the rationale for such military exercises. As detailed in Table 3.1, these operations focused mostly on scenarios involving non-conventional, non-state threats. However, very few reports focused on these types of threats to explain the justification behind these missions: unexpected events had to take place in order to venture in this direction. The most famous of these incidents certainly is the search-and-rescue mission following the crash of First Air flight 6560 near Resolute Bay on 20 August 2011. Coincidentally, operation NANOOK 2011 was about to take place in Resolute Bay and the scenario consisted of a simulated plane crash and the subsequent search-and-rescue mission. Henceforth, NANOOK participants were among the first to arrive on the scene, thus receiving credit for saving the only 3 survivors (12 were killed). Media coverage of the event made it a point to emphasize the crucial role played by CF personnel, an initiative echoed by the Prime Minister who commended them, pointing that their "quick response saved lives" (quoted in The National, August 23 2011). However, the coincidence also put the spotlight on the lack of year-round search-and-rescue capability in the North. All three news outlets had informed viewers that no search-and-rescue assets were located in the high Arctic, with two stations notifying their audience that the closest base for conducting such a mission in the Canadian Arctic was located in Trenton, Ontario. Harper admitted to such limitations: "we have to be realistic. There is no possible way, in the vastness of the Canadian Arctic, we could ever here have all of the resources necessary close by. It's just impossible" (The National, August 23 2011). Hence, the plane crash event was a reminder of Canada's erratic surveillance over the region, as well of its lack of political will to devote sufficient resources in order to manage it effectively. The crash of flight 6560 sporadically attracted media attention. However, operation NANOOK was justified in other ways.

Indeed, a state-centric perspective dominated media coverage of these operations. In the majority of reports, journalists communicated an often repeated message: global warming would reveal untapped natural resources and would turn the Canadian Arctic waterways into a maritime highway. With the sovereignty over the region being contested, state actors, especially the United States and Russia, were presented as the main obstacles to the achievement of sufficient Canadian control of the region. Reporter Rosemary Thompson encapsulated this by stating that

> Scientists believe that 25 percent of the world's untapped oil and gas is in the Arctic. That's why researchers are racing to map the Arctic Ocean floor to help buttress Canada's claim to the United Nations. But other countries like Norway, Denmark, Russia, and the United States will be staking claims, too. And their ships are now sailing more often in the Northwest Passage, now open part of the year because of global warming.
>
> (*CTV News*, August 19 2009)

Thompson went on to connect this depiction to the justification for operation NANOOK:

> we have seen the Russians use a submersible to plant their flag at the north pole under water, so today's exercise was designed to show the Russians and everyone else that Canada's military can operate in the Arctic, too.
>
> (*CTV News*, August 19 2009)

The interception of Russian fighter jets in close proximity to the Canadian airspace in 2010 reinforced this narrative:

> Defending northern sovereignty against foreign nations trying to claim it is the theme of Harper's Arctic tour. And in pure coincidence, the prime Minister revealed intruders were spotted just yesterday 30 kilometres from Canadian soil.
>
> (*CTV News*, August 25 2010)

As presented in Chapter 2, the above-mentioned military exercises allowed the CF to share their opinions on the desirability of these operations in the media. Out of 13 individuals interviewed in these televised reports, 7 were either retired or acting CF personnel. This helped cast these deployments in a positive light, with 9 individuals supporting the initiative and only one criticizing it (three were neutral).

Finally, journalists focused on governmental announcements, with Prime Minister Harper as the focal point, accompanied by local politicians and dignitaries in a press conference setting. This last category comprised most of the televised reports, as seen in Table 3.4.

Hence, governmental political messaging found great diffusion during these tours. Very little analytical reporting was done; reporters did

Table 3.4 Number of reports and average length of reports per category

	Start of trip	*Military exercises*	*Governmental announcements*	*Other*
Number of reports	8 reports	18 reports	49 reports	14 reports
Average number of words per types of report	309 words	294 words	338 words	427 words

not often venture outside of the tightly controlled and organized tours to cover other Northern social or economic realities, as the low number of reports in the "other" category demonstrates.

As a result, most of the airtime was centred on the Prime Minister and the scheduled announcements or activities. This provided a great platform for Stephen Harper to promote his Arctic initiatives. In fact, the Prime Minister was seen on screen an average of 15% of the time[4]; this also proved to be a strategic advantage for the Conservative government as their Arctic policy was deemed by opposition parties to be too militaristic and focusing too heavily on the military to enforce Canadian Arctic sovereignty. And certainly, as presented in this chapter, the military was made an intricate part of these tours, with Prime Minister Harper making numerous appearances alongside CF personnel. However, as presented in Table 3.3, only 2 out of 23 announcements made were of a military nature/focus. Economic (9), environmental (5), scientific (4) and social (2) investments by far outnumbered military ones. These high-profile trips represented great opportunities to influence popular perceptions of Conservative Arctic policy and to fend off the main line of criticisms of political opponents; Arctic policy was not solely about military initiatives. At the same time, economic and environmental investments fit perfectly with the remainder of the Conservative platform. Most economic initiatives were tailored to stimulate the development of Northern natural resources, and environmental ones sidestepped the climate change issue to focus on a conservationist approach. For example, three such announcements were about the creation or expansion of national parks in the Northern territories, whether on land or at sea. These non-military investments represented 45 out of the 49 televised reports on announcements.

As previously stated, Harper was the main protagonist in these stories, but not the only one. The same categories of experts described in Chapter 2 (academics, bureaucrats, civil society representatives, and elected representatives) were relied upon in these reports. Their opinions were sought after by reporters to add to the narrative or to help provide additional information and perspective. In fact, all individuals (other than Harper) interviewed for these reports monopolized 13% of air-time[5]. It should be added that different ministers (mostly Peter McKay but also John Baird, Leona Aglukkaq, and Michael Fortier) were also called upon for soundbites by reporters, thus reiterating governmental messaging.

In total, 91 individuals other than the Prime Minister were weaved into these news broadcasts. Many did not relay or criticize the government's Arctic agenda. They were sought upon by journalists to provide technical information (on the Franklin expedition, for example) or to describe logistical challenges (for operation NANOOK). Hence, 35 of these 91 interventions were considered neutral, neither supporting nor opposing Conservative Arctic initiatives.

Reporters allowed for critical voices to be heard, albeit in a minority status. Only 23 of these experts expressed criticisms, whereas 33 voiced supportive comments towards governmental Arctic policies. It is interesting to compile the identity of these individuals in order to describe the nature of the coalition for or against the Conservatives on Arctic issues. Critical voices were diverse: scholars, Inuit activists, and environmentalists formed the majority of these critical voices (12 out of 23). Moreover, it is interesting to note that these critiques were not concentrated in one particular broadcaster or even type of broadcaster (public vs private ones, for example).[6] In fact, 10 of these 23 criticisms were expressed at *CTV News*; hence there was only marginally more critical voices heard at public broadcasters than on private media.

On the other hand, supportive voices either emanated from retired or active CF personnel (10) or public servants from departments other than National Defense (5). Additionally, scholars (3), local elected representatives (3), and Conservative MPs had been sharing their opinions on air, although in a lesser frequency than public servants' interventions. Surprisingly, despite the at times acrimonious relations between the Conservative government and First Nations, three Aboriginal chiefs were supportive of Harper's strategy to facilitate the development of natural resources in the North.

Other than these actors, journalists could also voice criticisms towards government. Did they play a role of critique?

Reporters and journalistic objectivity

Generally speaking, reporters could not be considered as open critiques of these tours. However, as professionals professing allegiance to the journalistic ethic of objectivity, quite a few of them expressed critical opinions towards Harper's initiatives; close to 25% of TV reporters did so. However, these criticisms were less than overt. In many occasions, journalists claimed relaying critics issued by others, while at the same time not referring to specific critics ("critics say that"/"some were questioning"...). The "some people say" strategy is problematic because journalists can dissimulate personal opinions under the cover of relaying unspecified expert opinions.

Critical comments can be re-grouped in three categories. The first category comprises journalists who were adamant at pointing that investments took time to materialize and that many initiatives already announced were behind schedule. This had the effect of dampening the importance of announcements as these proved to be in some instances mere words without concrete follow-through. In the second category, journalists questioned the nature of the government's Arctic policy. Here, reporters pointed out that the Harper government adopted a militaristic approach to assert Canadian sovereignty and mentioned the timid environmental focus displayed by this same government. Finally, the most significant critique espoused the form of the photo-operation frame. Indeed, journalists covered the PM's every actions and announcements. However, 13 reports highlighted the photo-operation nature of the tours, and in doing so, debunked the idea that these trips were first and foremost to assert Canadian sovereignty over the region. Thus, this framing diminished the relevance of these tours by presenting them as partisan exercises meant to further electoral interests and gather positive media coverage. Radio-Canada reporter Emmanuelle Latraverse eluded to "mises en scènes aussi spectaculaires que minutieusement orchestrées" (*Le Téléjournal*, August 21 2009), whereas *CTV News* reporter Danielle Hamadjian called the tours "expensive, well-choreographed photo-ops" (*CTV News*, August 20 2012). CBC journalist Leslie Mackinnon used similar terms when she described Harper's visit of operation NANOOK 2009 as a "carefully choreographed photo-op" (*The National*, August 19 2009).

It must be noted that this framing was used more frequently in 2009 and 2010, when the Conservatives infused the tours with more partisan rhetoric. This in turn also coincided with Prime Minister Harper taking on a more participative role in the successive NANOOK operations, observing the operations first-hand rather than only addressing soldiers to inaugurate or close the operations. The 2009 tour attracted the most comments on this front. CF deployed air, naval, and land capabilities in operation NANOOK, with Prime Minister Harper at the forefront, arriving in a Sea King helicopter and landing on HMCS

Toronto. The 2010 operation mobilized a similar level of resources, with Harper arriving in a military chopper, with Coast Guard vessels in the background and CF-18s flying in the vicinity.

However, other photo-operations were much more successful in avoiding criticisms. Indeed, the PM's activities that carried a lighter tone received important media coverage while presenting Harper under a humorous or casual light: Stephen Harper spontaneously dancing with Native dancers and zooming on an all-terrain vehicle (2010) or going target-shooting with Rangers (2013). This presented the Canadian population with a more laid-back, lighthearted Prime Minister in contrast to his rather rigid exterior. As a result, senior correspondent Terry Milewski commented that "it's either an imposter or Harper is becoming just a bit unbuttoned" (*The National*, August 26 2010).

Conclusion

All in all, media coverage of these trips closely followed governmental agenda and facilitated for the most part governmental political messaging. However, they were not devoid of critical reflections (although not fundamental in nature) and presented a good balance of supportive and critical reactions to the government's Arctic plan. Media attention devoted to these tours increased with time, countering comments made by a reporter at the effect that these tours had lost their novelty appeal with time and had become somewhat of a habit, a routine (*Le Téléjournal*, August 26 2011). If such was the case, media coverage did not reflect this tendency. Covering governmental announcements was the main focus of televised reports, which rarely expanded beyond governmental messaging. Frames used by media outlets were closely related to governmental priorities and agenda.

Indirectly, televisual coverage supported governmental initiatives with the description of Arctic geopolitics eschewed by journalists. Many reports explained the relevance of these varied sovereignty-assertion initiatives by painting a grim portrait of circumpolar relations, one rooted in metaphors of race and confrontation. The race metaphor was widespread, with the idea that a race to claim Arctic natural resources was already underway. Competing claims by other sovereign states provided evidence that the region was up for grabs, and that others were eyeing Canadian Northern resources; everybody wanted a piece of the Arctic. The Russian threat was the most often cited by journalists. For example, the 2007 incident that saw a Russian expedition drop a flag at the bottom of the sea under the North Pole was mentioned from 2007 to 2009. China, Denmark, and the United States were also listed as states staking claims or coveting Northern resources. These assessments were made by reporters for whom the Arctic (or defence policy for that matter) was not an area of specialization. Many journalists who covered these tours were national affairs or Parliament Hill correspondents (think, e.g., Emmanuelle Latraverse or Terry Milewski).

This type of assessment was also usually undertaken by reporters so as to justify two types of governmental initiatives. First, it provided explanation as to why the Harper government championed the development of natural resources project in the North: facilitating resource development made sense since there was a race for resources. Second, these threats were cited as reasons to ensure control of the Canadian Arctic through the deployment of hard power capabilities in operation NANOOK. These exercises projected perceptions that Canada was able to enforce sovereignty on what it considered to be its national territory.

All in all, the media contributed to the success of these tours. Private and public broadcasters rarely took time to cover events outside of the ones prescribed by the acting government. Hence, public relations by government was effective, further explaining the positive voter intention effect created by these tours and reported by Landriault and Minard (2016).

Notes

1 The actual course was unknown but the most plausible route would have consisted of a straight line, going from the North Pole through the Nares and subsequently the Davis straits, near Ellesmere Island.
2 The typical tours usually began in Nunavut before going to the Northwest Territory and Yukon.
3 The third report offered an in-depth look at Arctic issues while also serving as an introduction for an in-studio discussion between two experts and the broadcast's host.
4 This figure was reached by adding the number of words pronounced by the Prime Minister in these reports (4,280 words) divided by the total number of words in all transcripts (31,040 words).
5 Taken together, these individuals represented 4,036 words in these transcripts out of a total of 31,040, hence 13% of airtime.
6 A persistent perception spread by the Harper government was that public broadcasters were constantly critical of the Conservatives, these institutions being dominated by people defending small-l liberal values.

References

Canadian Press. January 26 2006. Here Is a Transcript of Prime Minister-designate Stephen Harper's News Conference. The Canadian Press, Ottawa.
CTV News. August 20 2012. Harper. CTV.

CTV News. August 25 2010. Harper. CTV

CTV News. August 19 2009. Harper. CTV.

Delacourt, Susan and Andrew, Mills. December 14 2005. Bush Envoy Rebukes Martin. *Toronto Star*, p. A8.

Department of Foreign Affairs and International Trade. 2005a. *A Role of Pride and Influence in the World – Commerce* (last checked August 31 2016) http://publications.gc.ca/site/eng/9.666373/publication.html

Department of Foreign Affairs and International Trade. 2005b. *A Role of Pride and Influence in the World – Diplomacy* (last checked August 31 2016) http://publications.gc.ca/site/eng/272595/publication.html

Department of National Defence of Canada. 2005. *A Role of Pride and Influence in the World – Defence* (last checked August 31 2016) http://publications.gc.ca/site/eng/9.687487/publication.html

Gordon, Sean. December 23 2005. Harper Unveils Arctic plan. *Toronto Star*, p. A6.

Gorrie, Peter and Calamai, Peter. December 8 2005. Martin Fails to Budge U.S. *Toronto Star*, p. A6.

Griffiths, Franklyn. February 22 2006. Breaking the Ice on Canada–U.S. Arctic Cooperation. *Globe and Mail*, p. A21.

Harper, Stephen. August 10 2007. Prime Minister Announces Expansion of Canadian Forces Facilities and Operations in the Arctic. Prime Minister Office (last checked February 6 2017) http://webarchive.bac-lac.gc.ca:8080/wayback/20070814235713/; www.pm.gc.ca/eng/media.asp?category=2&id=1787

Ipsos Reid. September 4 2006. Majority (54%) Feel P.M. Was Wrong Not to Attend Recent International AIDS Conference (last checked March 17 2017) www.ipsos-na.com/news-polls/pressrelease.aspx?id=3176

Landriault, Mathieu. 2013. La sécurité arctique 2000–2010: une décennie turbulente? Ph.D. Dissertation, University of Ottawa (last checked February 6 2017) www.ruor.uottawa.ca/handle/10393/24353

Landriault, Mathieu and Minard, Paul. 2015. Does Standing Up for Sovereignty Pay Off Politically? Arctic Military Announcements and Governing Party Support in Canada from 2006 to 2014. *International Journal*, volume 71, issue 1: pp. 41–61.

Le Téléjournal. August 23 2013. Un journaliste chinois goûte à la médecine du premier ministre Harper. Radio-Canada.

Le Téléjournal. August 26 2011. Bilan de la tournée de Stephen Harper dans le Nord canadien. Radio-Canada.

Le Téléjournal. August 21 2009. Stephen Harper conclut sa tournée dans le Grand Nord canadien. Radio-Canada.

Le Téléjournal. August 19 2009. Stephen Harper dans l'Arctique: exercice militaire et médiatique. Radio-Canada.

Le Téléjournal. August 28 2008. Les défis de la souveraineté canadienne en Arctique. Radio-Canada.

O'Neill, Juliet and Cobb, Chris. August 18 2006. AIDS Issue Too "Politicized" to Announce New Funding Initiatives, Harper Says. *National Post*, p. A11.

The National. August 23 2011. Stephen Harper Flew to the High Arctic Today to Visit a Mourning Community. CBC.

The National. August 26 2010. Harper on an ATV: "I Make the Rules". CBC.

The National. August 19 2009. Discussion of Government's Arctic Sovereignty Agenda. CBC.

Wattie, Chris and Weeks, Carla. December 20 2005. U.S. Sub Visit Embarrasses Canada: Opposition. *Star Phoenix*, p. A9.

4 2010–2015

Arctic governance in a new era

If the early 2000s were characterized by the emergence and speculations around climate change in the Arctic region, the years that followed were tumultuous to say the least, especially in Canada. In fact, a succession of sovereignty incidents erupted from 2005 to 2009: a spat with Denmark about the ownership of Hans Island (summer 2005), a controversy around the transit of a US submarine (Winter 2005) and uproar over the drop of a Russian flag under the North Pole (Summer 2007) punctuated this tumultuous period. New players also entered the regional game. For example, the European Union pushed environmental-protection issues to carve itself a role in the region, advocating for an Arctic treaty mostly centred on environmental conservation and promotion of science (Shadian, 2013: pp. 274–7).

Alliances realignment and geopolitical dynamics were in a state of flux. This time period is defined as turbulent mostly due to the intense media coverage and partisan attention these developments received; for the most part, these crises did not have a material impact on Canada's Arctic claims. However, heightened public attention preceded initiatives undertaken by the Canadian government to have a more effective presence in and control over its Arctic.

As seen in Chapter 3, the Government of Canada led by Prime Minister Stephen Harper opted to make the Arctic a priority. Starting with the announcement to acquire six to eight Arctic/Offshore patrol ships in July 2007, Canada moved forward to dote itself with material capabilities so as to match rhetoric to action. Similar activism was observed in 2008 and 2009 with investments on a new icebreaker, funding to document Canada's claims on the continental shelf and the expansion of the Rangers program. Investments from 2010 to 2015 were centred mostly on social and economic programmes rather than military or typical sovereignty-assertion hardware means.

Arctic geopolitics also evolved and became more stable during the same time period. Multilateral forums, such as the Arctic Council, started to be perceived by states as venues conducive for establishing rules and promoting norms. In fact, according to professor Peter Hough, the Council went from being considered a high-level forum "to a fully-fledged intergovernmental organization with a permanent base and binding rules emanating from a decision-making process" (Hough, 2013: p. 103). Indicative of this kind of trend is the signature of agreements between sovereign states such as the one on search-and-rescue responsibilities, announced at the 2011 ministerial meeting of the Arctic Council. Agreements on criteria to accept new observers on the Council and the signature of the Agreement on Cooperation on Marine Oil Pollution Preparedness and Response consolidated this evolution in 2013. The fact that the Ukrainian Crisis, and especially Russia's involvement, did not produce significant spillover effects in the Arctic points to the special character of the region and the pragmatic cooperation between states and non-state groups.

At the same time, this period was characterized by a debate on the increased involvement of non-Arctic states in the region. The interest of many experts shifted from focusing on the Russian threat to evaluating the intentions and interests of China in the Arctic. Some experts, such as Michael Byers, adopted a conciliatory approach minimizing the danger posed by China to Canadian Arctic interests (Byers, August 29 2011: p. A11). Others, such as Rob Huebert and David Wright, rang the alarm bell and warned Canadians of the contradictions between Chinese and Canadian interests in the Arctic (Wright, 2011; Lackenbauer et al., 2018: pp. 8–13). The issue that gathered the most attention in media coverage and governmental political messaging was centred on the inclusion or exclusion of non-Arctic states as observers on the Arctic Council. A security discourse on China's Arctic policy remained relatively contained in comparison with the attention devoted to the resurgence of Russia and its Arctic policy and interests, especially from 2007 to 2010. No event exposure involving China was comparable to the coverage given to the 2007 drop of a Russian flag at the bottom of the sea under the North Pole.

Public opinion shifted as well during this era. The polls sponsored by the Munk–Gordon Arctic Security Program in 2010 and 2015 provided evidence of changing public attitudes. The main conclusion one can draw from these two polls is that advocates of holding a firm line against other states were fewer in numbers in 2015 than in 2010. When asked which strategy their country should follow on border and/or resource disputes, only 36% of Canadian respondents chose the option "My country should pursue a firm line in defending its sections of Arctic territory regardless of the cost," down from 43% in 2010 (Gordon Foundation, 2015). In contrast, more participants thought that Canada should seek a negotiated compromise with other countries on border or resource disputes in the Arctic. A similar pattern was observed when participants were questioned on the necessity to strengthen military presence for protection against international threats: support for such an option went from 58% in 2010 to 48% in 2015.

Awareness of the Arctic Council also seemed to have an impact on support for one of these strategies. Indeed, respondents who had clearly or vaguely heard about the Council were more likely to prefer a diplomatic outcome to Arctic border and resource disputes (50%) in comparison to individuals who had not heard (39%) about the multilateral organization (see Figures 4.1 and 4.2).

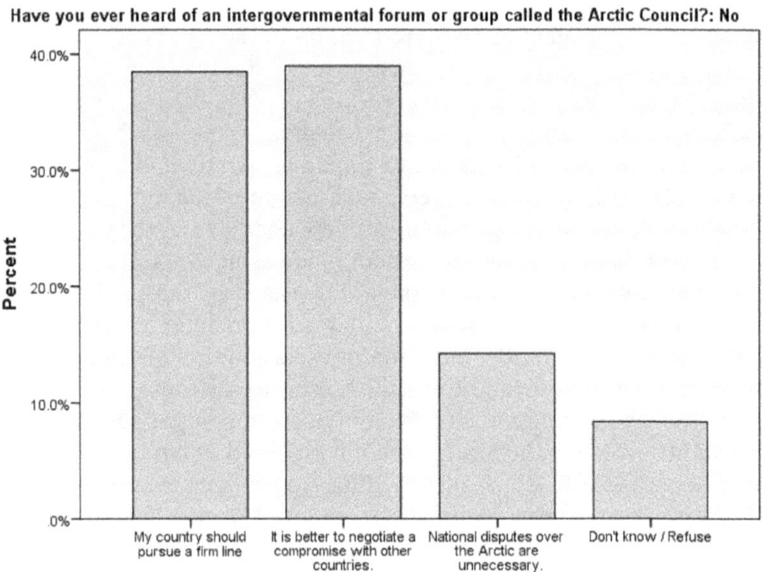

Figure 4.1 Preferred approaches towards resource and border dispute and levels of awareness of the Arctic Council in the 2015 edition of the Rethinking the Top of the World poll.

Note: This first graph (Figure 4.1) illustrates preferred approaches to Arctic borders and resources disputes for respondents not cognizant of the Arctic Council.

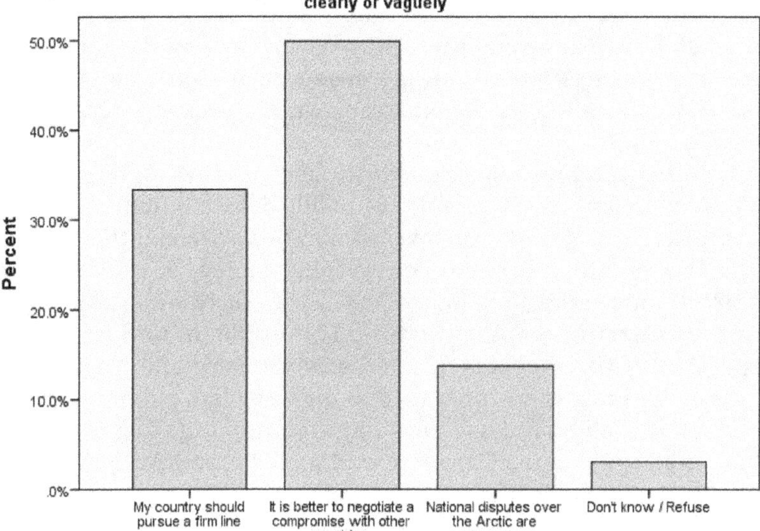

Figure 4.2 Preferred approaches towards resource and border dispute and levels of awareness of the Arctic Council in the 2015 edition of the Rethinking the Top of the World poll.

Knowledge of the Council made respondents not only more likely to refuse non-Arctic states having a say in Arctic affairs (+5%) but also more likely to adopt a conciliatory approach towards Russia. For example, only 29% of respondents who had heard about the forum were supportive of suspending Arctic cooperation with Russia as a result of the Ukrainian conflict. On the other hand, 45% of subjects who were not aware of the multilateral organization agreed to suspend Arctic cooperation with Russia.

Overall, it would appear that the Canadian populace was not very anxious about its Arctic, favouring non-violent means, such as negotiations, to govern this region. Awareness of multilateral arrangement in the region also seems to impact support for diplomatic solutions. Consequently, the media could affect how Canadians perceive the Arctic region; information about Arctic governance and multilateral forums as well as media attention can strengthen cognitive association. The objective of this chapter is to determine if media coverage had an influence on this change in attitudes. Media attention can influence popular awareness about these issues; the nature of the attention, however, must be scrutinized to better decipher the nature of the content to which Canadians were exposed. A cursory look at the number of references to Arctic sovereignty in Canadian newspapers points in the direction of a calmer media landscape with regards to Arctic issues (see Figure 4.3).

Arctic sovereignty concerns, which caused many sovereignty crises, were no longer at the centre of public debate or making headlines after 2010. In fact, the overall noise on sovereignty declined after that point. At present, however, the content of such noise is of great importance to help denote whether there was a change of focus or narratives on Arctic issues. This would, in turn, allow the analysis to further concentrate on how the slow and progressive governance process was presented to the Canadian public. In order to reach this objective, one must pay attention to the issue frames that were at play in the Canadian media on Arctic governance during the period studied.

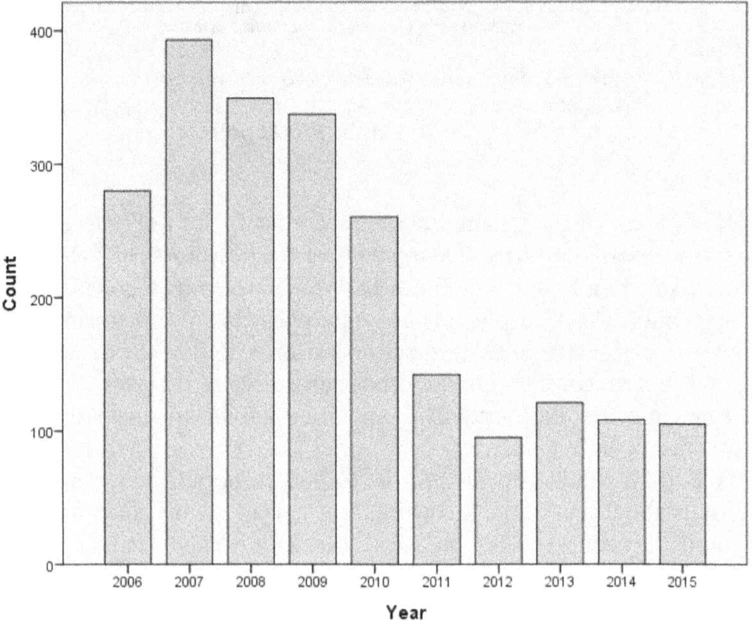

Figure 4.3 Number of articles published in Canadian newspapers containing the mention "Arctic sovereignty" from 2006 to 2015.

The unspectacular nature of governance

The concept of governance defines this period well. Governance is typically associated with political processes that display three elements: first, the involvement of a multiplicity of stakeholders trying to reach an objective. Second, these actors are not all governments: many types of decision-makers (companies, civil society, governments) are involved and participate in putting in place rules and frameworks in which actions and policies can take place. Finally, governance is about coordinating efforts from these different actors; as such, the level of control and predictability in policy outcome is reduced (Ruhanen et al., 2010: pp. 5–6).

Arctic politics took on many forms and were articulated at different levels of government, involving a multiplicity of actors, both private and public. The Arctic Council was, and still is often posited as the primary forum dealing with Arctic governance but there are other venues, such as the Arctic Circle assemblies, that connect government officials, experts, business leaders, and indigenous representatives. Most of them, however, often flow under the media radar. For the purpose of analyzing media coverage, this chapter will focus on key meetings held at the Arctic Council. The presence of high-level ministers or officials heightened the status of the Council, with the signature of agreements increasing media attention.

Three events will be studied. First, the focus will be on the ministerial meeting of the Arctic Council held in Nuuk in May 2011, given that this search-and-rescue agreement was officially announced at this meeting. The second event of interest will be the ministerial meeting of the Council held in Kiruna, Sweden, in May 2013. Indeed, a second agreement was announced at Kiruna (the marine oil pollution prevention agreement) while Canada also assumed chairmanship (2013–2015) of the Council at this meeting. Finally, media coverage of the Senior Arctic officials meeting of the Council at Yellowknife in March 2014 will be scrutinized. This meeting is quite interesting as it occurred immediately after the annexation referendum held in Crimea on mid-March and right in the midst of the Ukrainian Crisis at a time when potential for conflict and disagreement was obvious between Western countries and Russia.

Representations of the Arctic region follow specific patterns, and typologies re-group these representations into images projecting specific understandings about the region. Steinberg et al. (2014) provided interesting analytical insights to help study media coverage of Arctic governance more efficiently. While analyzing media framing present in member and observer states of the Council, Steinberg et al. isolated two recurrent images: northern protectionism and global interconnectedness. It seems that both frames share common themes while articulating opposite priorities: "both shared the common themes of natural resources, shipping routes, climate change, and international political status, but framed them along different lines depending on whether international interest was seen as welcome or threatening" (Steinberg et al., 2014: p. 279). Furthermore, the Northern protectionism frame focused on the national character of the Arctic region, defining it as "a space of national development and resource wealth" (Steinberg et al., 2014: p. 280).

In contrast, the global interconnectedness frame emphasizes on scientific and political collaboration, labelling the region as "a space of connection and commerce" and opportunities (Steinberg et al., 2014: p. 281). It must be noted that both frames have been tested in the Rethinking the Top of the world poll, with the firm line (northern protectionism) and negotiated compromises (global interconnectedness) options on the preferred approach to broader/resource disputes.

Nonetheless, one important frame is missing. Indeed, many civil society actors (indigenous groups, environmental non-governmental organizations) perceived emerging Arctic phenomenon (shipping, resources, and so on) as threatening, akin to the Northern protectionist frame. However, these actors do not reify national identity or development. On the contrary, this frame presents national control of the Arctic as problematic and advocates for additional environmental protection to counter an increased presence or development of resources in the Arctic region. Hence, from this perceptive, more national control may not necessarily constitute the solution. This frame will be referred to as the global commons frame.

Steinberg et al.'s study represents the most thorough examination of media representations on Arctic politics; this being said, it does contain two serious limitations for our purpose. For one, the breadth of countries covered had an impact on depth. Merely a few articles per country were analyzed: for example, only 20 news articles from the Canadian media were scrutinized. Additionally, while the authors attempted to represent languages accurately (French and English for Canada, e.g.), the authors conceded that the sampling selected was not perfectly representative. Indeed, the selection appears odd for Francophone publications, with some articles from *Les Affaires* and *Le Soleil* referenced, but none from *Le Devoir* or *La Presse*, two of the most popular francophone newspapers in Canada.[1]

The other shortcoming of this study has to do with the vagueness of the measurement applied to the reporting pieces. Indeed, both issue frames may be present in the same news article; hence, a more detailed distinction of which is dominant (in terms of words) would then be in order. Furthermore, the method used by the authors on this point is not clear, indications pointing to the fact that each article was either considered as belonging to one framing or the other. The lack of clarity does not end there. While the researchers stressed that "Canadian and Russian news coverage strongly emphasized the national character and identity of the Arctic region" (p. 279), no specific quantitative observation was made to make this statement more precise.

This chapter has for ambition to fill in these gaps for the Canadian media by providing quantitative observations and by delving deep into each news article to understand how the three issue frames were used and the relative popularity of each.

Canadian media and Arctic governance

Two televised media (CBC and Radio-Canada) and 15 newspapers[2] were included in the sample studied. In total, 61 reports were published or broadcasted just before or right after the Arctic Council meetings[3] in 2011, 2013, and 2014.

The 2013 Kiruna meeting attracted the most amount of media attention by far, representing close to 60% of the sampled reports. Hence, it would seem logical to begin by scrutinizing media coverage for this summit, especially since Steinberg et al.'s study solely focused on this event. Overall, Steinberg et al.'s conclusions are not replicated. In fact, opposite observations are reached for the Canadian media's coverage of the Kiruna meeting: the global interconnectedness frame dominated all other frames. More specifically, the global interconnectedness frame constituted the main issue frame in 70% of reports and garnered 50% of all attention devoted to the meeting (see Table 4.1).

Table 4.1 Use of different frames by the Canadian media before, during, and after the 2013 Kiruna meeting

	Global interconnectedness	*Northern protectionism*	*Global commons*	*Total*
Number of stories in which the frame is dominant	25	6	5	36
Number of words	11,117	4,882	3,395	19,394
Average % of total story	51	22	16	89%[4]

It must be noted that while northern protectionism did circulate to interpret the 2013 meeting, it did so in a minor fashion. As seen in Chapter 1, real-life developments must be present in order for specific interpretations to be deployed. In this case, opposition to the European Union being granted observer status at the Council may very well just be what partially explains the use of this frame. The use of this issue frame here may be attributed to the nomination of Leona Aglukkaq as Canada's representative to the Council. The minister of Health was an outspoken defender of Inuit people and Northerners, chastising Southerners mistakes in the North. As narrated by reporter Paul Koring,

> Ms. Aglukkaq is especially irked by outsiders telling Arctic peoples what should happen in their homeland. She tartly dismisses Olivier De Schutter, the UN special right-to-food envoy, as "a hypocrite" for failing to back the seal hunt. And she is infuriated by groups like the Humane Society of the United States that raise millions annually railing against a white-coat seal pup hunt that hasn't existed for decades. "I'm fighting to keep our meals on the table, I'm fighting a global community to defend my right to seal meat or the polar bear," she says. "It's a challenge but as a Northerner and an Inuk person that depends on the environment I live in, I have a lot to contribute."
>
> (Koring, May 11 2013: p. A12)

This pro-Northerner stance was present in most articles covering Aglukkaq's nomination as Canada's lead person at the Arctic Council. Denigration of scientists was also part of the rhetoric, with Aglukkaq criticizing the "gaggles of scientists who flock north in summer" and "expert outsiders whose claims didn't stand the test of indigenous knowledge" (Koring, May 11 2013: p. A12). Environmentalists were also targeted by this northern protectionist discourse, with reporter Paul Koring stressing that Aglukkaq "already served notice that she's fed up with southern environmentalists trying to dictate – or stall – northern development" (Koring, May 15 2013: p. A8).

On the other hand, the Conservative government's main Arctic initiative during the Kiruna summit was to pitch the idea of putting in place an Arctic Business Forum that would grant a more substantial role to businesses in developing Northern economies. In itself, this idea constituted a global interconnectedness initiative, trusting corporate actors to bring positive economic gains from commercial endeavours in the Arctic region. Acceptance of non-Arctic states as observers and an agreement to improve oil spill responsiveness added to the spread of the global interconnectedness frame by reaffirming the high level of cooperation in the circumpolar region.

The global commons frame came in third place as this position was not relayed by any governmental officials. The actions undertaken by non-governmental organizations such as Greenpeace or the Arctic Athabaskan Council accounted for the overwhelming majority of such occurrences.

The 2011 Nuuk and 2014 Yellowknife meetings received a similar media treatment, albeit in a less intensive fashion than the Kiruna meeting. Again, the global interconnectedness image was the preferred perception, far outnumbering the two other frames for the 2011 meeting (see Table 4.2).

The signature of an international treaty dealing with search-and-rescue areas of jurisdiction significantly influenced the results for the Nuuk gathering. Preliminary discussion on ways to prevent and react to oil spills in the Arctic region were also frequently reported in the Canadian media. The cooperative spirit that animated state-to-state discussions in May 2011 was reflected in media reporting.

The release of a joint declaration on resource development by Inuit organizations contributed to elevate the status of the global commons frame. In the words of Jimmy Stotts, president of the Inuit Circumpolar Council – Alaska, "we're not convinced, at least in Alaska, that it's

Table 4.2 Prevalence of different frames used by the Canadian media before, during, and after the 2011 Nuuk meeting and the 2014 Yellowknife meeting

	Global interconnectedness	*Northern protectionism*	*Global commons*	*Total*
Number of stories in which the frame is dominant (2011)	15	2	3	20
Number of words (2011)	5,287	1,596	1,963	8,846
Average % of total story (2011)	51	15	19	85%[5]
Number of stories in which the frame is dominant (2014)	3	2	0	5
Number of words (2014)	657	914	0	1,571
Average % of total story (2014)	40	55	0	95%

sustainable so far, despite statements that are made by government or industry or others" (cited in *CBC News*, May 12 2011).

The observation that political developments seem to drive media frames is noteworthy. The 2014 Yellowknife meeting is the only one during which northern protectionism was more prevalent in terms of words. The assertive attitude of the Government of Canada towards Russia as a consequence of the Ukrainian Crisis was reflected in media accounts. Ministers Lisa Raitt and Leona Aglukkaq promoted the governmental line in media interviews, highlighting the need to adopt a tough stance towards Russia, including on the Arctic file.

One more observation should be stressed, this time related to a non-event: almost no mention of disputes of sovereignty or boundaries were made in these reports. Contrary to the 2000–2010 era when any crisis or issue would seem to spark a national sovereignty conversation, institutional cooperation acted as a powerful deterrent for conjuring the Arctic conflict image. A few mentions were made of a competition for Arctic riches and resources, usually in the context of the inclusion of non-Arctic states (especially China) as observer of the Arctic Council. Most of these mentions were not clear, however, on whether the interest of the states was a positive or negative development, an opportunity or a threat.

These Canadian results do not represent a striking contrast with the international press coverage of the same events. For example, *The Economist* published only one article in reaction to the 2013 Kiruna summit (The Economist, May 18 2013: p. 67). The global interconnectedness frame was the dominant interpretation present in the report, with 60% of the article displaying this frame against 40% putting forth the northern protectionist frame. Similar coverage was also observed in *The Economist* for the periods between Arctic Council meetings. The global interconnectedness frame was in full display, downplaying sovereignty concerns and emphasizing interdependence, as can be seen in this passage:

> Reassured that they have little to squabble over, Arctic countries are finding that the enormous costs of research, policing and energy exploration are better shared. Hence, for example, the eagerness of Russia's state-owned energy companies to form joint ventures, such as that agreed last year between Rosneft and Exxon Mobil in the Kara Sea. The development of Arctic shipping-lanes will also be made easier with good regional relations: there is talk of either Iceland or Norway developing a transshipment port to serve Russia's north-eastern route.
>
> (The Economist, March 24 2012: p. 61)

Overall, it would seem that the global interconnectedness frame prevailed over other issue frames in televised and printed reports (these accounts had for primary objective to report current events and focus on the day's news). Other media, such as Maclean's, which publish on a weekly basis, tend to look at the long-term picture and often mix analysis and in-depth reporting: longer articles provide interesting material and stray away from the minutia of daily developments.

"The Arctic has never been hotter"

Maclean's reporter Luiza Savage's article entitled "Why the world wants the Arctic" is worth dissecting to better understand how these three frames were displayed. The article was published on 8 May 2013, in anticipation of the Kiruna summit.

Two frames, northern protectionism and global interconnectedness, were used by the author, whereas the global commons frame was notably absent. Savage opened her article by establishing a well-known narrative: the Arctic region was in the midst of global transformation. Stressing that "in geopolitics, the Arctic has never been hotter" (Savage, 2013: p. 18), the author went on to describe the opening of new shipping lanes and unlocking of new resources and riches. The description of China's rising activism in the region was used to portray a "fraught moment of growing global interest," tying the knot of a definite northern protectionist introduction (Savage, 2013: p. 18).

After briefly alternating between the global interconnectedness and northern protectionist frames, Savage presented Canadian reluctance to accept non-Arctic states as observers on the Arctic Council. Here again, Leona Aglukkaq was interviewed in length, expressing fears that the new players around the table (especially the European Union) would sideline Northerners or hurt them. The minister also attacked the global commons frame, stressing that the Arctic was not Antarctica and should not have been treated as a national park. As with other media reports, the northern protectionist frame was balanced by the pro-business priority of the Harper government, and the emphasis put on "organisations that actually are developing the North – the mining industry, cruise ships, fishing industries" (Savage, 2013: p. 18). Agreements signed at the Arctic Council also constituted evidence of this global interconnectedness frame. However, the same type of process described in Chapter 2 of this book was utilized again. The perspective rendered evident in Savage's introduction was re-applied in the conclusion, with the author warning that "with that open border come concerns about organized crime and illegal trafficking in drugs and people" (Savage, 2013: p. 18). Set against a backdrop of military build-up in Russia and Alaska, and the Arctic Council not habilitated to tackle national security or military issues, it was made clear that this "completely new era" we were entering in Arctic governance is one fraught with dangers and competition between state interests.

All in all, the northern protectionism frame dominated this article, accounting for 57% of the article against 32% for the global interconnectedness frame. More surprisingly, Savage's article used many of the narratives (shipping lanes, new riches, illegal trafficking, and military build-up) that were very prevalent before 2010 but almost absent in media reports covering Arctic Council meetings. A more thorough investigation is needed so as to analyze media coverage in-between these Arctic Council meetings, both in dailies and periodicals.

A more limited sample was drawn in order to limit queries and produce specific results on Arctic governance. Three dailies (*Globe and Mail*, *Toronto Star*, *National Post*) with different editorial lines and owners were selected for study as well as two periodicals (Maclean's and L'Actualité). The search parameters covered from June 2011 to April 2013, with a focus on the period between the Nuuk and Kiruna meetings, and from 18 May 2013 to 25 March 2014 so as to cover the time period between the Kiruna and Yellowknife meetings. In total, 33 articles were published in dailies and 8 in the sampled periodicals.

The almost complete disappearance of sovereignty claims mentions and boundary disputes was again observed for the periods between these meetings. Five articles mentioned sovereignty issues, with three of those focusing on the continental shelf issue and two on the Northwest Passage (NWP) dispute. Most of these stem from a strategy by the Harper government to get its message across. In an interview granted to the *Globe and Mail* in January 2014, Prime Minister Stephen Harper was outspoken about his opposition to "efforts to grant influence to outsiders" in the region,

> To be blunt about it, I think, frankly, this had already gone way too far before we became government, but given that's the precedent that's been established… we're prepared to have a significant number of observers as long as they understand and respect the sovereignty of the permanent members and as long as their presence doesn't override or impede upon the deliberations of the permanent members.
>
> (Harper cited in Chase, January 17 2014)

Harper went a few steps further, accusing the people not supporting this frame of being enemies who oppose Canadian sovereignty. In his words,

> I think it's important for Canadians to understand that this view - that our Arctic should be internationalized - does exist in some academic and bureaucratic circles. People who criticize what we're doing in our North are doing so because this is in fact their real view. They're not complaining about our government having a sovereignty agenda merely because they don't like military investments. They may not like them. But they're actually complaining for a deeper philosophical reason: They actually don't support Canada's sovereignty in this area.
>
> (Harper cited in Chase, January 18 2014b: p. A13)

In this same interview, the Prime Minister formulated dubious sovereignty claims, claims that would have been vehemently criticized had they emanated from Russia, for example. Harper combined claims on the North Pole defended by Canada in the 1930s with more recent international law regimes, namely, regulations structuring the process to delimitate the extent of the continental shelf as codified in the United Nations Convention on the Law of the Sea (UNCLOS). Following the UNCLOS, scientific evidence had to be gathered to support such extension, making the process a science-driven, technical assessment. Harper noted a continuity from the 1930s to the present regime, observing that

> Canadian governments have claimed the North Pole since at least the 1930s. So there would have to be a compelling reason to surrender that claim. There is no such compelling reason. The view of the government, as a whole, is that at this stage we should make the maximum claim we can make, plausibly and with scientific evidence.
>
> (Harper, cited in Chase, January 18 2014b: p. A13)

The thoughts of the Prime Minister were relayed in three different articles published on 17 and 18 January 2014. Another article, published on 21 January, dealt with the reply of the Chinese state to the Prime Minister's interview, through the reaction of spokespersons from China's ministry of Foreign Affairs and Chinese scholars. However, this type of political messaging stood as the exception rather than the norm; Harper's interview acted as a singular burst of sovereignty during a rather calm period for Canada's Arctic policy. It represented an anomaly bearing no important consequence as the interview was granted in January 2014, eight months after the inclusion of many non-Arctic states as observers on the Arctic Council.

This also highlights the relatively low salience given to the Arctic file by the Conservative government. The Arctic served a strategic purpose on the Conservative government's agenda, allowing the Prime Minister to defend a nationalist cause without constituting a contradiction with the broader governmental orientation:

> It allows him (Harper) to tweak American noses, but do it on a file where he can't be accused of anti-Americanism. It's not a criticism of capitalism, the West or liberal democracy or free enterprise.
>
> (Chase, January 18 2014a: p. A12)

The interest for the Arctic file was short-lived but to back away from key initiatives, such as the annual summer Prime Ministerial tour of the Arctic (see Chapter 3), would have resulted in detrimental consequences:

> It was largely politically driven at the beginning, and then he was intent to keep doing them so it wouldn't be dismissed as something Southerners do as a once-or-twice, window-dressing thing [...] To be frank, he can't stop doing them now. It would be very symbolic.
>
> (Chase, January 18 2014a: p. A12)

From sovereignty to governance, from Russia to China

In all actuality, the most dominant approach was to downplay sovereignty threats and to highlight the scarce use of the use-it-or-lose-it rhetoric in circumpolar relations in general and Canada's Arctic policy in particular. One sole article made the classical review of sovereignty disputes that Canada was facing: written by reporter Steven Chase, the article is a sober and balanced portrayal of sovereignty issues, pointing out that "realistic threats to Canada's ownership in the North are small" (Chase, January 18 2014a: p. A12). On the other hand, "Canada [...] has an opportunity to claim expanded seabed rights to potential energy and mineral resources in the polar region" (Chase, January 18 2014a: p. A12). Chase also brought to light challenges faced by residents of the High Arctic, from infrastructure to economic development and food issues.

Only three articles among those studied focused extensively on Russia's Arctic policy, constituting a peripheral interest for the Canadian media. The focus on specific states may also partially explain this scarcity. This level of attention contrasted with the media treatment of the Russian threat after the drop of a Russian flag at the bottom of the sea, under the North Pole late July 2007. The move, inserted in the broader narrative around the resurgence of Russia on the international scene, sparked a period of intense media coverage of Arctic affairs, mostly from 2007 to 2010 (Landriault, 2016). However, this also sparked sovereignty dominated discussions in which the issue of the continental shelf occupied a central place; Russia, as an Arctic power, was thought to aggressively pursue an expansionist policy via the collection of evidence to document its continental shelf case.

China replaced Russia as the main preoccupation in media coverage of Arctic affairs from 2011 to 2014. Indeed, the Asian country was front and centre in four articles and mentioned in passing in six others. This focus on China served to illustrate growing patterns in the region, namely, of an Arctic Council growing in influence and importance and of the introduction of non-Arctic states in the regional governance structures. Coverage on China's Arctic involvement was fairly balanced and presented nuanced assessments. For example, reporter Nathan Vanderklippe did not succumb to the excesses illustrated in Chapter 2. When describing the potential for Chinese shipping in a more open Arctic region, Vanderklippe was cautious:

> how many Chinese ships might sail those waters, however, remains unclear - the Arctic, after all, is a hard place to operate, with a limited shipping season and unpredictable weather that can wreak havoc on schedules that need to be kept.
>
> (Vanderklippe, January 20 2014: p. A8)

The article concluded, quoting Professor Frédéric Lasserre, that China's interest in Arctic shipping was extremely theoretical. This China focus shifted media attention away from sovereignty disputes to concentrate instead on governance issues for which the two main concerns revolved around resource exploration and shipping.

The emphasis on resources and shipping did not emerge during this period; it had been raised many times from 2000 to 2010. However, the discussion on these two issues was mostly theoretical and vague. The most common assessment in the latter years of the 2000s was that a rush to Arctic resources was inevitable and that Arctic shipping lanes would see increased traffic in the near future, sparking competition and conflict between states to ripe these benefits (Landriault, 2013).

This idea was expressed in many journalistic reports from 2011 to 2014, although mentions of tensions, conflicts or regional instability were only present in a small minority of texts. This narrative usually is the departure point of these articles. Journalists have referred to Arctic geopolitics as the 21st century version of the Great Game (Koring, September 2 2011: p. A4), the race to the riches of the Far North (Waldie, October 17 2013: p. B1) or as an Arctic invasion (Sorensen, 2013: p. 32). Journalistic interest then focused on evaluating their own claims and debunking their own construction: is an invasion imminent? Will a rush be witnessed?

The 2011–2014 period provided elements of answers to these questions and journalistic coverage provided a balanced and thorough evaluation of interests for Arctic resources and shipping lanes. In total, 10 articles had such assessments as main focus: serious doubts were expressed in seven of these ten reports, with only three reinforcing the invasion scenario.

The transit of the cargo ship *Nordic Orion* through the NWP during the Fall of 2013 could have sparked rhetorical inflation as it was the first commercial bulk carrier to navigate through the NWP. This precedent could have inflamed the media sphere, and created a flurry of articles analyzing the prospect of shipping through the NWP. And yet, only two articles mentioned the transit specifically, spurring an evaluation of the potential of shipping in the Canadian Arctic. In both cases, insurance costs were presented as the principal obstacle deterring shipping companies from using Northern passages, stressing that the risk was extreme (Chase, January 22 2014: p. A4) or that the Arctic represented a "difficult and expensive place to do business" (Sorensen, 2013: p. 32).

All in all, the attitude that prevailed was one of restraint. The vast majority of experts cited in these reports were also of this opinion. For example, Frédéric Lasserre observed that "the maritime traffic in the Northwest Passage increases but more slowly that what was forecasted 10 years ago" (Lasserre cited in L'Actualité, February 1 2012: p. 7). A similar attitude was adopted by a corporate executive from the shipping industry cited by reporter Steven Chase who remarked that "he doesn't believe Arctic sea routes will carry much volume in the next 15 to 20 years" (Chase, January 18 2014a: p. A12).

The Arctic region was presented in its complexity and regional particularities rather than as a unified space that experienced the same extent of changes brought by climate change. This represented the most refreshing evolution in media coverage and was another sign that the use-it-or-lose-it outlook had lost steam during this time period. Indeed, one of the fundamental characteristics of the use-it-or-lose-it perspective was to consider the Arctic as a uniform region without taking sub-regional specificities into account (Bartenstein, 2010).

As such, global warming and the melting of the ice cover was often presented during the 2000–2010 time period as a phenomenon that would impact the entire Arctic region as a whole. Evidence on the extent and the nature of the melt helped to underline a crucial distinction between the Russian and Canadian Arctic, the Northeast and Northwest Passages. With its shorter routes, the Russian Arctic offered more opportunities to the shipping industry and for Asian states to reach European markets. Increase in maritime traffic through the Northeast Passage was reported with caution so as to point out that this pattern could not be observed in the Canadian Arctic (Sorensen, 2013: p. 32; Chase, January 22 2014: p. A4; Vanderklippe, January 20 2014: p. A8).

A similar assessment could be noted for reports centring on Arctic resources. As with shipping, allusions to a race to riches generating tensions and conflicts were (and still are) a staple of journalistic reporting. However, the race and conflict imagery did not always correspond to reality, leaving journalists to develop conflicting stories. For example, *National Post* reporter Adullah Hussain observed that "Canada may have to wait a little while longer, as oil majors focus on other opportunities," and concluded that "most of it (the oil and gas potential) may not see the light of the long Arctic days anytime soon" (Hussain, July 20 2012: p. FP7). The author expanded on the many obstacles slowing Arctic resources extraction: lack of political will, environmental liabilities, low oil and gas prices, and domestic jurisdictional problems. Even while listing a litany of reasons to conclude that Arctic resources were not a panacea, Hussein referred to this subject as a "global race for Arctic resources" and pointed out the economic boom that was underway as a result of this race:

> Towns and communities across the vast Arctic landscape are waking up to the riches that lie buried beneath, as oil executives scope for prospects and Arctic governments take another "strategic" look at the region's hydrocarbon and mineral riches.
>
> (Hussein, July 20 2012, p. FP7)

In an article published in the *National Post* on 13 February 2013, reporters Yereth Rosen and Gladys Fouche for their part downplayed the conflict frame, citing the region as one of political stability and where "border disputes between the eight politically stable states of the Arctic Council are peaceful," with its isolation offering security against potential maritime threats (Rosen and Fouche, February 13 2013: p. FP3). This stability was listed as the main reason for oil companies to eventually return to Arctic waters, "drawn by political stability and shallow waters." The reporters went on to cite that an estimated $100 billion would be invested in the next decade, mostly in the oil and gas extraction sector.

The era of Arctic governance

The Canadian media deployed different frames during this time period. Of course, unsubstantiated or vague allusions to a race for resources did not completely disappear, but were greatly reduced in number and balanced by counter-evidence. Sovereignty disputes typically have the potential to create crises, with political leaders as protagonists exchanging warnings, and partaking in grandstanding and chest thumping around themes of identity and nationalism. Arctic governance, on the other hand, seems to derive from another logic – one interested in the day-to-day minutia of administrating and governing policy issues with interested stakeholders. Civil society and companies are key actors in this process and the concerns are usually of a more pragmatic nature.

While sovereignty disputes usually centre on ownership and have an inherent zero-sum game attached to them (to possess or not possess), governance does not result in an all-or-nothing outcome; applicability of rules and the reaching of a pragmatic and (often technical) objective are the desired outcomes. In terms of resources, this might mean accumulating data to understand the particularities of the Arctic environment as well as evaluating the feasibility of resources exploration and extraction. As far as shipping is concerned, shipping companies are more interested in navigating these (largely) uncharted waters safely and securely than making a grand statement. In either case, it is difficult to sensationalize decisions and programmes that are typically carried out in terms of years, not days; these dilemmas and debates are not conducive to perform agenda-setting.

Governance is harder to cover from a media perspective, leaving even seasoned reporters with a complex situation hardly subsumed in a tight word limit and deadlines. This results in the adoption of a state-centric approach with important media attention directed towards covering organizations led by sovereign states, even with organizations that follow governance processes (the Arctic Council, e.g.). Emerging forums, such as the Arctic Circle Assembly, the Northern Forum or Arctic Frontiers, involve different types of actors (e.g., companies, environmental associations, indigenous communities, scientists, and governmental representatives). These gatherings are also part of Arctic governance, with interested parties being active stakeholders. A focus on organizations like the Arctic Council favour the use of frames highlighting cooperation and coordination among Arctic stakeholders. As Arctic states decided to use the Arctic Council to develop treaties and agreements, media coverage followed suit.

As can be seen in Table 4.3, media coverage for Arctic meetings still overwhelmingly favours a state-centric institution (the Arctic Council) rather than organizations centring on non-state actors (such as Arctic Frontiers or Arctic Circle, e.g.), at least in Canada's reference newspaper (*Globe and Mail*). A local news outlet (*Nunavut News*) did not fare particularly better on this front.

Social media platforms (Twitter, e.g.) also put more emphasis on forums such as the Arctic Council, especially when agreements are reached by member states. However, they offer a flexible platform for emerging forums to promote their activities. Hashtags referring to the Arctic Council meetings gather more tweets than those referring to meetings held by other forums. In turn, these expose the plurality of actors present in the Arctic region, helping to construct a more complex understanding of the Arctic.

The reliance on social media to acquire information has increased exponentially in the past decade. Hence, it would only seem logical to inquire how Arctic issues are covered in popular social media: do they represent a definite break with traditional media practices?

Table 4.3 Number of mentions of each organization in the *Globe and Mail* and *Nunavut News* (in brackets) from 1 January 2013 to 31 December 2017

Mentions of organizations	*2013*	*2014*	*2015*	*2016*	*2017*
Arctic Council	23 (16)	19 (17)	9 (10)	2 (6)	4 (4)
Arctic Frontiers	1	0	0	0	0 (1)
Arctic Circle	0 (3)	1	0 (1)	0	0 (1)
Northern Forum	1 (2)	0	0	0	0

Notes

1 The list of all articles used for the content analysis is incomplete in the research article, with the only articles quoted being listed in the reference list.
2 These are: *Calgary Herald, Chronicle Herald, Edmonton Journal, Globe and Mail, La Presse, Leader Post, Le Devoir, Montreal Gazette, National Post, Ottawa Citizen, Star Phoenix, Telegraph Journal, The Province, Toronto Star, Vancouver Sun*.
3 The exact periods covered are as follows: 9–14 May 2011, 13–17 May 2013, and 26–27 May 2014. Editorials were excluded to focus on journalistic reporting, ensuring uniformity in format and objective.
4 Some passages could not be counted as belonging to any of the three frames; these were discarded as neutral description of events or actors.
5 Some passages could not be counted as belonging to any of the three frames. These were discarded as neutral description of events or actors.

References

Bartenstein, Kristin. July 1 2010. "Use It or Lose It": An Appropriate and Wise Slogan? *Policy Options*, available at http://policyoptions.irpp.org/magazines/immigration-jobs-and-canadas-future/use-it-or-lose-it-an-appropriate-and-wise-slogan/

Byers, Michael. August 29 2011. Asian Juggernaut Eyes Our "Golden" Waterways. *The Globe and Mail*, p. A11.

CBC News. May 12 2011. Arctic Council Leaders Sign Rescue Treaty, available at www.cbc.ca/news/canada/north/arctic-council-leaderssign-rescue-treaty-1.1049847.

Chase, Steven. January 22 2014. Polar Shipping Code Takes Shape. *Globe and Mail*, p. A4.

Chase, Steven. January 18 2014a. Nationalism, Northern Style. *Globe and Mail*, p. A12.

Chase, Steven. January 18 2014b. We Should Make the Maximum Claim We Can Make. *Globe and Mail*, p. A13.

Chase, Steven. January 17 2014. Harper Wary of Rush to Arctic. *Globe and Mail*, p. A1.

Gordon Foundation. April 22 2015. Rethinking the Top of the World: Arctic Public Opinion Survey, volume 2, available at http://gordonfoundation.ca/app/uploads/2017/03/APO_PowerPoint_Volume-2_WEB.pdf

Hough, Peter. 2013. *International Politics of the Arctic – Coming in from the Cold*. Routledge, London.

Hussain, Adullah. July 20 2012. Left Out in the Cold? *National Post*, p. FP7.

Koring, Paul. May 15 2013. Canada's Aglukkaq Readies for Hot Seat at Arctic Council. *Globe and Mail*.

Koring, Paul. May 11 2013. Leona Aglukkaq's Personal Arctic Stake. *Globe and Mail*, p. A12.

Koring, Paul. September 2 2011. Canadian Icebreaker Joins the Polar Parade. *Globe and Mail*, p. A4.

L'Actualité. February 1 2012. Destination Nord. *L'Actualité*, volume 37, issue 2: p. 7.

Lackenbauer, P. Whitney, Lajeunesse, Adam, Manicom, James and Lasserre, Frédéric. 2018. *China's Arctic Ambitions and What they Mean for Canada*. University of Calgary Press, Calgary, Alberta.

Landriault, Mathieu. 2013. La sécurité arctique 2000–2010: une décennie turbulente? Doctoral Thesis, University of Ottawa, Ottawa, ON.

Landriault, Mathieu. 2016. Interest and Public Perceptions on Canadian Arctic Sovereignty: Evidence from Editorials, 2000–2014. *International Journal of Canadian Studies*, volume 54: pp. 5–25.

Rosen, Yereth and Fouche, Gladys. February 13 2013. Land of Stable Politics and Shallow Water – Despite Risks, Shell Will Return to Drilling in the Arctic – and It Won't Be Alone. *National Post*, p. FP3.

Ruhanen, Lisa, Scott, Noel, Ritchie, Brent and Tkaczynski, Aaron. 2010. Governance: A Review and Synthesis of the Literature. *Tourism Review*, volume 65, issue 4: pp. 4–16.

Savage, Luiza. 2013. Why the World Wants the Arctic. *Maclean's*, volume 126, issue 20: p. 18.

Shadian, Jessica. 2013. The Arctic Gaze: Redefining the Boundaries of the Nordic Region. In S. Sörlin (ed.) *Science, Geopolitics and Culture in the Polar Region*. Ashgate, Surrey: pp. 259–89.

Sorensen, Chris. 2013. Frozen Out. *Maclean's*, volume 126, issue 44: p. 32.

Steinberg, Philip, Bruun, Johanne and Medby, Ingrid. 2014. Covering Kiruna: A Natural Experiment in Arctic Awareness. *Polar Geography*, volume 37, issue 4: pp. 273–97.

The Economist. May 18 2013. A Warmer Welcome. *The Economist*, volume 407, issue 8836: p. 67.

The Economist. March 24 2012. Cosy Amid the Thaw. *The Economist*, volume 402, issue 8777: p. 61.

Vanderklippe, Nathan. January 20 2014. For China, Looking North Is a New Way to Go West. *Globe and Mail*, p. A8.

Waldie, Paul. October 17 2013. Looking Up: The Far North's Global Appeal. *Globe and Mail*, p. B1.

Wright, David. 2011. The Panda Bear Readies to Meet the Polar Bear: China and Canada's Arctic Sovereignty Challenge. *Canadian Defence and Foreign Affairs Institute*, available at https://d3n8a8pro7vhmx.cloudfront.net/cdfai/pages/42/attachments/original/1413673951/The_Panda_Bear_Readies_to_Meet_the_Polar_Bear.pdf?1413673951

5 Social media, Arctic tourism and the Crystal Serenity

The increase of maritime traffic in the Arctic region brought forth a diverse array of issues. As covered in Chapter 4, shipping and resources issues attracted the bulk of attention from the media, national governments and international forums. Concerns over possible oil spills, commercial bulk shipping, and potential usage of the Northwest Passage (NWP) were frequently mentioned in typical threat assessments of Canada's security and sovereignty in the Arctic region.

However, a warmer Arctic would also equate to increased maritime traffic for reasons other than resource exploration/extraction and shipping goods. The melting of glaciers acted as a novel destination for tourists attracted by pristine natural landscapes and a breathtaking flora and fauna, a phenomenon known as last chance tourism (Eijgelaar et al., 2010; Dawson et al., 2010; Lemelin et al., 2010). On this regard, the melting Arctic can be compared to other world destinations that are threatened to disappear because of the forces unleashed by climate change and global warming. As suggested by Lemelin et al., the Arctic is faced with the same predicament as the Great Barrier Reef, Mount Kilimanjaro, or the Everglades (p. 477). Likewise, Polar Regions have usually been analyzed together in the academic literature, as they faced similar challenges, opportunities, and dilemmas (Snyder and Stonehouse, 2007a; Lück et al., 2010; Stonehouse and Snyder, 2010).

These dilemmas connect with some of the more pressing questions asked during the 1969 Manhattan transit and the Prime Minister's annual Arctic tours: they also comes at a time of transition in Arctic governance. First, touristic operators are relatively new players in the Arctic region, emerging from this new era of governance focusing not so much on state actors, but rather on private or non-state actors. Second, heightened public awareness of the consequences of global warming produced a surge in tourists motivated to visit soon-to-be vanished attractions before it is too late. Hence, the connection with media coverage is a direct one: the more the populace is made aware of the imminent danger of the global melt and its impacts on the Arctic environment (and especially, specific species, such as the polar bear), the more it is likely to attract last-chance tourists.

Finally, the media landscape has been in transition as well. Traditional media have for the most part been struggling, losing their audience at the expense of new, online media. Consumers have been migrating to online platforms to stay informed as well as to express their opinions and react to current events. As a result, traditional media have been scrambling to choose a strategy to remain profitable amid high costs, a multiplication of new news providers recycling content and/or making it free to their readership. This emerging trend and its impacts on Arctic coverage must be scrutinized in order to decipher if new media represents a break or continuity with traditional media coverage. But first, it is imperative to figure out the patterns and dilemmas raised by Arctic tourism.

Arctic tourism: trends and dilemmas

Arctic tourism has only recently begun to generate great public or academic interest. It must be stressed that the relatively low number of touristic expeditions offered in Canada's Arctic can explain the initial disinterest. Academic and public attention has been overwhelmingly devoted to one main type of tourism: cruises. As Stewart and Dawson (2011: p. 263) highlighted, although the first cruise in the Canadian Arctic dates back to 1984, we had to wait until 2006 to observe considerable growth in this sector, with 22 cruises offered during the whole year.

A surge of tourism was noted from 2006 to 2010 in both Polar Regions and all Arctic countries, with subsequent years experiencing important drops. Factors coming both from the supply (lack of ice-strengthened vessels capable of navigating Canadian Arctic waters) and demand (recession) sectors explained this boom-and-bust cycle. Tight Canadian regulations and a lack of infrastructures (especially ports) also provided explanations for this lack of interest on the part of cruise operators, rendering the prospect for future expansion bleak (Lasserre and Têtu, 2015). The 2006–2010 era was a time of great media interest in the Canadian media, which receded in the years that followed; this boom-and-bust model mirrored the pattern observed for Arctic tourism (Landriault, 2013, 2016).

As with any type of human activity, tourism has the potential of generating both positive and negative repercussions. The bulk of academic attention was directed towards assessing whether Arctic tourism engendered more harm than good as far as economic, environmental, and social impacts were concerned. For example, many cruises framed the trips they offered as a chance to become more familiar with the impact of climate change by having a first-person account of the ravages caused by global warming. The thought process hints that such a trip could raise awareness and lead individuals to become activists once they returned to their communities. Eijgelaar et al. (2010) found that such purported awareness effect was minimal for cruises visiting Antarctica. These tourists fell in the category of "polar mass market tourists," being more interested in comfortable sightseeing and accommodation (p. 347). In total, 77% of surveyed tourists by Eijgelaar and his colleagues did not change their opinions on climate change as a result of their trip.

The lack of social impact must be put in relation with the high environmental costs associated with such cruises, given that "polar cruises produce some of the highest per capita CO_2 emissions in tourism" (Eijgelaar et al., 2010: p. 340). Researchers also discovered that only 7% of respondents said that they had (or planned to) offset their emissions. Similar results were found by other researchers when calculating social awareness impacts and greenhouse gas emissions for the polar bear sightseeing industry in Churchill, Manitoba; carbon cost was high for marginal awareness payoffs (Dawson et al., 2010). Cruises also produced other types of environmental consequences: the air pollution, sewer, wastewater and solid waste disposals produced by these large vessels; crew and guests are additional elements included in the environmental harm column (Stonehouse and Snyder, 2010: pp. 110–3).

Of course, not all expeditions are of the same nature and yield the same output. For example, the Students on Ice (SOI) program has for main objective to educate young people on social and environmental realities of Polar Regions, leading to participants with greater awareness (Green, 2010: pp. 93–105). Adventurers must also be distinguished from cruise passengers. These types of tourists typically boast a smaller ecological footprint (Orams, 2010: pp. 13–22) and share areas of convergence with local inhabitants, especially on their relationship to nature (Grimwood, 2015).

On the other hand, the economic impact of Arctic tourism on local communities has proven more difficult to decipher. We know, however, that it generates revenues and ensure jobs. According to Snyder, tourism accounts for 13,000 full-time jobs for Indigenous people living in Northern Canada (Snyder, 2007a: p. 103). About 500 people across Nunavut work in the tourism industry, with an additional 3,000 people actively working in the arts and crafts sector, which represents an integral part of tourism in the territory (Robbins, 2007). However, this economic sector comes with its down sides. As described by Snyder (2007b),

> The host community bears virtually all the costs of constructing, operating and maintaining the port facilities and other infrastructure needed to serve the ships and their passengers. Another economic disadvantage is that locally owned businesses must compete fiercely with the cruise ship for tourist expenditures.
>
> (p. 56)

Studies on the economic impact of Arctic cruises for local communities are rare, with typical economic assessments focusing rather on industry trends and the number and destination of cruises and the growth potential for operators (Stonehouse and Snyder, 2010; Lasserre and Têtu, 2015).

Respect for local cultural heritages also constituted an area of concern in the academic literature. On this regard, touristic endeavours were evaluated on their respect for local inhabitants and their cultural practices and beliefs, especially with regards to the indigenous people living in the North (Grimwood, 2015). Impact on local communities was perceived as particularly salient to assess since tourism activity in the Canadian Arctic generates a situation where tourists are more numerous than a region's local inhabitants. The necessity of relying on a community-based approach to deal with this issue is usually underlined in order to manage the costs and maximize the benefits out of the increased development of the tourism sector (Kajàn, 2013). According to Stonehouse and Snyder (2010), this can translate into mutual benefits:

> Cultural groups that want to participate in polar tourism, whether Inuit, Saami or Alaskan Native, determine what aspects of their cultural resources will be shared, how they can authentically be represented, and where and when tourism may occur. Strengthening is manifest in the resurgence of traditional languages and customs, initiatives taken in passing favourable legislation, protection of heritage sites and the wide acceptance of culture and heritage tourism by native communities.
>
> (pp. 128–9)

Lastly, safety issues were high on the policy agenda. The Arctic region brings forth a difficult environment that only elevates the risk of ships running aground and/or hitting floating ice, with an elevated risk of vessels sinking. This scenario brings forth questions concerning the capabilities of the Canadian government to lead search-and-rescue missions in a distant and vast territory, making this issue a wicked policy problem (Pincus, 2015). Precedents of ships running aground are listed as indications of potential risks that operators are facing (Klein, 2010). The grounding of the Clipper Adventurer, in August 2011, is one such incident that raised concerns about search-and-rescue capabilities in Canada (Stewart and Dawson, 2011).

These different areas of academic investigation lead our analysis to four possible issue frames concerning Arctic tourism: the economic benefits frame, the environmental impact frame, the local culture frame, and the safety hazard frame. However, one more frame needs to be added, this time related directly to the case at hand, the 2016 and 2017 Crystal Serenity cruises in the Canadian Arctic: the luxury frame.

Crystal Serenity cruises

Cruises and touristic expeditions typically only capture the attention of the public when something goes wrong or an incident happens (think the Clipper Adventurer in 2010, e.g.). However, the *Crystal Serenity* caught the public's imagination without the occurrence of unfortunate/accidental events. The operator, Crystal Cruises, organized the first voyage for the *Crystal Serenity* during the summer of 2016, after two years of planning and organization. Consultations with local inhabitants and precautions to reduce harm to the environment and fauna were also undertaken by the company through initiatives such as the use of distillate fuel instead of heavy fuel (Comer et al., 2016) and avoiding marine protected areas (McWhinnie et al., 2018).

The Crystal Serenity had more than 1,000 passengers and 600 crew on board. The vessel departed from Seward, Alaska on 16 August 2016 and reached New York City on 16 September. The 32-day voyage took tourists through the NWP and the Canadian Arctic, with the help of an icebreaker to open the way. The cruise ship also stood out for its luxury branding, with the price point for tickets starting at $22,000 (Orlinsky and Holland, September 8 2016).

The gigantic and luxurious nature of the Crystal Serenity embodies our final possible issue frame. As such, the cruise shared similarities with the 1969 Manhattan transit. In both cases, Canadians were presented with a precedent, whether a tanker or a massive ice-strengthened cruise ship. Furthermore, both vessels were impressive in size in comparison with similar vessels that operated in the Arctic region. Finally, in both instances, the economic gains were weighted against possible environmental harms to assess whether the voyages were worthwhile for Canadian Northern inhabitants and environment.

The novelty element around the cruise ship is only truly captured through a dissecting of the fundamental dynamics of tourism in the Canadian Arctic. Indeed, the Crystal Serenity introduced the era of mass tourism to the Canadian Arctic, which was dominated up to that point by smaller cruises making multiple expeditions a day (Lasserre and Têtu, 2015: p. 30). However, the cruise ship was also representative of a persistent trend in which more cruises began transiting through the NWP from 2006 to 2010. On this regard, the Crystal Serenity was not an exception but rather a continuation of an already well-established pattern (Stewart and Dawson, 2011: pp. 263–4).

Nonetheless, the expedition prompted calls to update Canadian legislation in order to ensure that touristic activities were held in a responsible and sustainable fashion. Such changes were requested at both federal and territorial levels (Dawson et al., 2017: p. 75; Government of Nunavut, October 2016; World Wildlife Fund, December 9 2016). Capitalizing on the success of the 2016 voyage, Crystal Cruises decided to go forward with a second edition in 2017. The company decided to halt the Arctic expedition after the 2017 edition until 2019, when smaller vessels would be scheduled to replace the Crystal Serenity (Zak, September 22 2017).

The traditional media and the Crystal Serenity transits

The main objective of this chapter is to describe social media coverage of the two transits. However, a first look at traditional media perceptions of the voyages is imperative in order to analyze whether traditional and social media offer a different interpretation of the events.

The time period covered ranges from two weeks before the transits to two weeks after the arrival to port.[1] Pre-travel hype and post-factum analysis could then be added to the coverage of the transit itself. Multiple media sources were included in the analysis: televised reports on Radio-Canada's *Le Téléjournal*, CBC's *The National*, CTV's *CTV News* as well as 12 newspapers composed the sample.[2] The terms "Crystal Serenity" have been used as keywords in order to limit the results produced by the search as to focus on the most relevant documents.

In total, 34 journalistic reports described the Crystal Serenity voyage. The media coverage was far from sustained during the whole time period, with close to 75% of reports published either at the start of the trip (early August) or at the time that tourists disembarked on the tiny hamlet of Cambridge Bay (late August). Media attention was tenuous in mid-August and in September.

Media coverage in traditional outlets paid little attention to the luxury frame while rather emphasizing on the disruption (or absence of) on local communities (see Figure 5.1).

The local culture frame monopolized journalistic focus. Media attention centred on the travellers' interests in local culture, traditions, and lifestyles as well as the possible disruption the voyage could produce in local communities visited. The collaboration and coordination between the company and the local communities were noted by reporters. The economic angle was mostly positive as it showcased an economic boon for local artisans and guides provided by the arrival of wealthy tourists. In both cases, reporters relied heavily on interviews with locals instead of experts or academics to document these dimensions. For example, Vicki Aitoak's point of view was showcased in numerous reports as she was the head of the Cambridge Bay welcoming committee. Very few Northerners interviewed raised fundamental or one-sided criticisms of the cruise ship; balanced and pragmatic opinions prevailed.

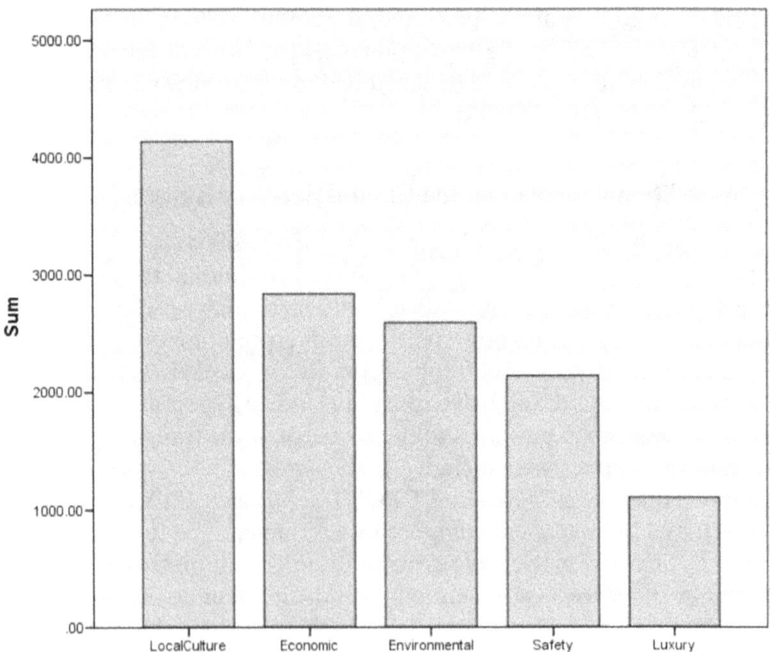

Figure 5.1 Number of words per frame when describing the Crystal Serenity transits in Canadian traditional media.

As for the other frames, the safety angle received a balanced treatment as both risks and possible hazards were described while retaining an emphasis on the high level of preparation of the crew. The precautious approach adopted by the company helped alleviate safety concerns, even though the perils of conducting a possible rescue operation for 2,000 people were raised by journalists. The environmental frame was overwhelmingly negative. While a minority of media reported the precautions taken by the Crystal Serenity (especially the use of low-sulphur diesel and the disposal of garbage), a majority of them underlined the damaging environmental impact on the Arctic environment and the planet. As Michael Byers explained in the *Globe and Mail*,

> larger ships such as the Serenity could accelerate the area's destruction [...] It's the nature of the exercise, which is to take a large cruise ship with a very large carbon footprint to the Northwest Passage to take advantage of the melting caused by climate change.
>
> (Byers cited in Migdal, August 20 2016: p. A6)

The company was also solicited by the media to share their point of view. For example, Crystal Cruises' spokesperson defended the limited ecological footprint resulting from the expedition or the lengthy collaboration exercise (three years) with local communities (Migdal, August 20 2016: A6; Weber, September 19 2016: A6). Naturally, the operator framed the tour in a positive fashion, hinting at an ecological awareness effect. As Crystal Cruises Vice President John Stoll stated:

> I think the interest is overwhelming. I think that anytime you present something that's new, something that people haven't done, when you can take a luxury audience, introduce them to expedition, it's rare. And the more that we can expose them to this part of the world, the more we think we're doing the job that we need to do. There shouldn't be limits. We shouldn't not expose our guests to some of the most remote places in the world. They want to see it.
>
> (Stoll cited in *CBC News*, 2016)

Nonetheless, the company was not able to voice its opinion widely in the Canadian media. Indeed, the company's representatives were only interviewed in 4 of the 34 media reports analyzed.

The luxury frame was not a popular one, as it was absent from 60% of all reports. When it was present, it usually occupied a minor portion of the article or clip, making it one of the top two frames in only 5 reports out of 34. However, it is interesting to note how the terms used to describe travellers were not flattering, to say the least. The Crystal Serenity vacationers were called "jaded tourist," "filthy rich tourist," "the world's worst people" (all three on CBC, citing the magazine *Slate*), travelling on a "rich palace" and that vacationers represented either a "hord" or an "invasion of tourists" (Postmedia Network newspapers) in small communities. The Crystal Serenity occupants were described as "peppering locals" with questions and "flooding" towns with sightseers.

Journalistic narratives combined frames to highlight debates or areas of tension arising from mass tourism (see Table 5.1).

Many articles solely listed different interrogations on the transit without articulating them together. These reports typically enumerated concerns and opportunities with very little effort to present them as trade-offs.

However, other journalists explicitly pitted one frame against another. For example, prospects of economic gains were most often weighted against disruption of local communities and harm to the environment. On both accounts, the economic advantages for local communities were deemed significant, whereas media outlets were adamant at stressing the efforts undertaken by Crystal Cruises to minimize social and environmental damages.

Finally, the event acted as a catalyst for initiating discussions concerning other related Arctic issues. Climate change, both on its scientific and human dimensions, Canadian sovereignty, Canada–US relationship in the Arctic and Arctic socio-economic development were issues all addressed while referring (albeit briefly) to the Crystal Serenity.[3]

Table 5.1 Frequencies of the top two frames in terms of words per article

Top two frames/report	*Number of occurrences*
Economic and local culture	10
Economic and environmental	9
Environmental and safety	5
Safety and luxury	3
Environmental and safety	1
Environmental and local culture	1
Local culture and safety	1
Economic and safety	1
Local culture and luxury	1

The most common observation was a familiar one for seasoned Arctic observers: the voyage would open an era of increased accessibility to the region, this time with mass tourism and luxury cruises. For example, readers of the *Ottawa Citizen* were informed that "the arrival of the Crystal Serenity ushers in an era of mass tourism made possible by increasingly ice-free summers" (Hopper, August 30 2016: p. 1). A similar observation was made in a majority of media reports, even though the peak of Arctic tourism happened to be years prior, between 2006 and 2010. As such, the popularity attached to this frame reminds the careful reader of similar observations made during the transit of the Manhattan (see Chapter 1) or from 2000 to 2005: the Arctic rush metaphor was still alive and well during the Crystal Serenity voyages, especially the 2016 edition.

Real-life developments and new information running in opposition to this recurrent narrative did not receive significant attention from the news media. As described earlier, Crystal Cruises decided to suspend its Arctic cruise in order to build two smaller cruise ships for future expeditions, thus undermining the "mass tourism is coming" image. No major Canadian dailies reported the company's move, leaving the story to be covered by specialized blogs and local (Northern) newspapers.

Additionally, the coverage of the Crystal Serenity voyages provides valuable insights into the changing nature of the media landscape. Indeed, it highlighted important concentration of media ownership and the accompanied consequences on media coverage of remote areas. Newspapers owned by Postmedia Network (*Calgary Herald, Edmonton Journal, Leader Post, Montreal Gazette, National Post, Ottawa Citizen, The Province, Vancouver Sun*) published the same three articles (two on August 2 2016 and one on August 30 2016), accounting for 65% of all reports. This resulted in high content homogeneity and impacted the diversity of perspectives and opinions.

Now, let us turn to social media in order to evaluate if social media diffuse different frames than traditional media.

From traditional to new media: academic challenges

So far, television and newspapers have been the main focus of interest. Newspapers provide a relatively well-structured media, amenable to academic scrutiny as the organization of the information is stable. Additionally, multiple databases render accessible decades of content, ranging from local to national newspapers.

On the other hand, the instantaneity of social media and their rather ephemeral nature render this scientific endeavour more perilous and uncertain: the scarcity of academic articles focusing on social media in Canada is illustrative of this hesitation. However, their popularity in the Canadian populace is undeniable, forcibly prompting us to adapt our analytical methods to figure out this emerging tool of communication.

Indeed, the number of Canadian users of Twitter has tripled in less than a decade, going from about 6% in 2009 to 20% by 2017 (Small, 2011: p. 875; Statista, 2018). Of course, the nature of the use of social media is quite different from one user to the next. However, strong evidence suggests that Canadians utilize different social media for different purposes. For example, Facebook has been adopted by many to share personal information, with close friends or family members. On the other hand, Twitter, one of the most popular micro-blog platform worldwide, has for main purpose information-sharing of current events to networks larger than family and friends (Grudz and Roy, 2014).

Users capitalize on the interactivity and the customization provided by the platform, turning their Twitter accounts into people-based newsfeeds (Small, 2011). By 2013, the internet was the second media source for Canadians to follow news and current affairs (Statistics Canada, 2016).

Social media introduced novel elements, changing the media/audience relationship by turning once-passive audience into active participants. It is unclear, however, whether traditional power relations once typical of the media landscape evolved or were ultimately transformed by this empowerment. Studies have shown that multiple influential actors in the communication and public relations business have made the transition by incorporating social media tactics and practices into their general communication strategy (see Bajkiewicz et al., 2011; Waters and Jamal, 2011; Dubois and Gaffney, 2014; Lachlan et al., 2016). In the case of corporations, social media allow them to diffuse unfiltered messages about their corporate actions and purposes (Bajkiewicz et al., 2011; DiStasio and Bortree, 2012).

Hence, Twitter is not a perfectly levelled playing field; traditional power holders in Canada (such as traditional media and politicians) retain their power on Twitter (Dubois and Gaffney, 2014), thus sparking the conclusion that the role played by Twitter is more reactive than proactive in nature. Indeed, trends and proclamations in traditional media tend to be repeated on Twitter (Murthy, 2015). In other national contexts, non-governmental organizations and politicians were also found to use Twitter to further their interests, although the impact they have is variable (Waters and Jamal, 2011; Adi et al., 2014). It should be added that even actors with similar partisan and ideological inclinations do not adopt similar or even cohesive strategies in their social media use.

Furthermore, Dubois and Gaffney also observed that bloggers and commentators emerged as influential people, even when they were not considered traditional power holders. Civil society groups, such as grassroots movements and political advocacy groups can gain notoriety by providing additional information to users and complementing traditional media (Himelboim et al. 2013).

The jury is still out assessing the impact that Twitter has on political dynamics in Canada and abroad. For one, it was found that the social media platform does not act as a catalyst for meaningful conversation (Small, 2011; Waters and Jamal, 2011; Grudz and Roy, 2014). Furthermore, Grudz and Roy (2014) concluded that Twitter creates limited pockets of open cross-ideological interactions as people tended to interact with people sharing similar opinions, creating an echo chamber effect. Moreover, the interactions between users from different ideological worldviews often led to confrontation, furthering political polarization.

These various findings were reached by studying tweet content published with a specific hashtag as hashtags are currently known as the best way to organize the voluminous content published every day on Twitter.[4] These hashtags were quite general, dealing mostly with national affairs (#cndpoli) and/or highly salient political phenomenon (#elxn41 for the 2011 federal elections). It will be interesting to see if these findings are applicable to more specific subject matters. For the purpose of this chapter, the hashtag #CrystalSerenity will be utilized to detail social media coverage of the cruise ship 2016 and 2017 voyages.

A cruise ship, in 140 characters

The same timeline used for traditional media (1 August 2016–30 September 2016; 1 August 2017–30 September 2017) was applied for analyzing Twitter. Only tweets written in French or English were retained, whereas tweets that were off-topic but nevertheless used the #CrystalSerenity hashtag were removed from the sample.[5]

In total, 404 tweets were written using the said hashtag. The same pattern could be observed when comparing both years. The 2016 voyage caught public attention (362 tweets), whereas the 2017 edition escaped the public's sonar (42 tweets); the "precedent" component clearly had an impact generating a buzz for the first edition. The overwhelming attention in 2016 can be explained by international interest rather than a purely Canada driven one. If 62% of tweets in 2017 were from Canadians, this proportion dropped to 44% for the 2016 trip: American and European users were active in 2016 while being for the most part passive in 2017.

On the other hand, coverage proved to be more constant on Twitter when compared with traditional media outlets. In 2016, tweets were written every day from 1 August to 17 September with the exception of a single day (14 August). However, similar interest peaks can be noted as tweet activity experienced a slight increase in mid-August before significantly peaking at the end of August. Much like traditional media, this latter peak occurred at the time that the cruise ship was to dock in Canadian Northern communities, first in Ulukhaktok (27 August) and Cambridge Bay (29 August). Here, social media trends mirrored traditional media, with many tweets sharing reports recorded by CBC reporter Chris Brown.

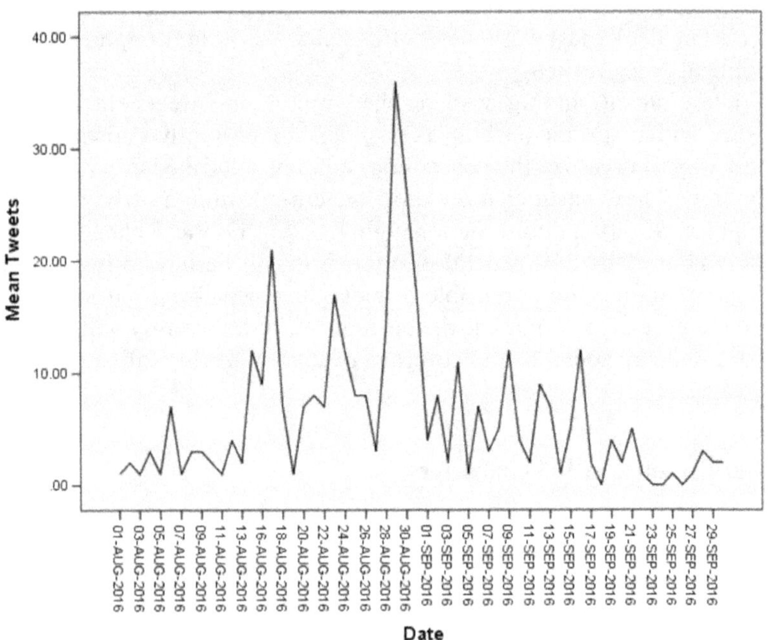

Figure 5.2 Frequencies of tweets per day in August and September 2016 under the #CrystalSerenity hashtag.

The influence of traditional institutions such as the traditional media and non-governmental organizations should be stressed. Only 14 tweets broke the 10 retweets barrier, all of which coming from handles with significant social capital, whether as a traditional media (e.g., the CBC or the Nunatsiaq News), a non-governmental organization (Ocean Conservancy), or a specialized news feed (Sea Trade Insider). These organizations constituted 42% of the sample, thus representing a sizable portion of the platform's coverage of the voyages.

The content of the tweets presented some analytical limitations. In most instances, authors did not take positions or deploy any of the frames described previously. However, users would retweet or share content created by other external sources. In fact, 30% of tweets displayed this practice. Therefore, the frame analysis was also extended to the resources shared by users.

Overall, there were approximately three times more tweets or shared links describing the voyages as positive compared to tweets presenting the cruise as negative.[6] This can be partially explained by the fact that cruise ship passengers participated in this effort, diffusing positive messages about their experience, the nature and people they encountered during the voyages. Many such positive reviews originated from accounts specializing on cruises, and especially luxury ones; these handles were considered to have very high levels of popularity as their number of followers were in the tens of thousands.

Comparing Canadians with other users allows us to better focus on Canada's social media landscape. Differences between Canadian and non-Canadian users were significant on some regards, whereas other aspects produced similarities. Indeed, twice as more dominantly negative tweets came from non-Canadians, meaning that the majority of critiques emanated from beyond Canadian borders (Table 5.2).

Non-Canadians also had the potential to influence others as their followers were typically more numerous than those of Canadian accounts. Differences in diffusion potential were linked to the type of user. Organizations, whether research institute or non-governmental organizations, have an established network of support, people dedicated to communications and relevant expertise on the subject matter. Thus, they have the means to mobilize members or sympathizers to their viewpoint and share the organization's point of view. On the other hand, Canadian users were typically individuals, with a smaller following; they were more likely than non-Canadians to remain neutral

Table 5.2 Perceptions, practices, and status of Twitter users who were active on the #CrystalSerenity, by national status

		Tweets by Canadian users (184 in total)	*Tweets by non-Canadian users*[7] *(220 in total)*
Type of user	Individual	117 (64%)	116 (53%)
	Organization	67 (36%)	104 (47%)
Popularity	Low (under 1,000 followers)	73 (40%)	61 (28%)
	Intermediate (1,000–3,000 followers)	73 (40%)	67 (31%)
	High (3,000–5,000 followers)	5 (2%)	35 (16%)
	Very high (Over 5,000 followers)	33 (18%)	56 (25%)
Dominant perception of voyages	Positive	86 (47%)	99 (45%)
	Negative	20 (11%)	49 (22%)
	Neutral	78 (42%)	72 (33%)
Link to other media	Yes	48 (26%)	74 (34%)
	No	136 (74%)	146 (66%)

and less likely to share links to other media. A greater number of individuals commenting could mean that they would add novel frames or highlight different frames than traditional media, participating in a democratization of the messages transmitted through social media platforms like Twitter.

Similar framing was performed for the perceived historical nature of the trips. A dominant frame consisted in stating that the cruises had inaugurated an era of mass tourism to the Arctic region. Considerations for respecting local communities, their culture and customs also ranked first in social media topics. In fact, the local culture (89 tweets), environmental (81), and safety (73) frames were all widely disseminated on the social media platform. While user opinions were predominantly positive about the respect of local culture and communities, they were more critical about the environmental impacts engendered by the trips. On the other hand, they were more ambivalent regarding safety concerns. For example, many users highlighted the inherent dangers and numerous hazards of navigating through the Canadian Arctic. However, an equal number of people enumerated the precautions taken by the company and expressed a reassuring opinion about safety concerns.

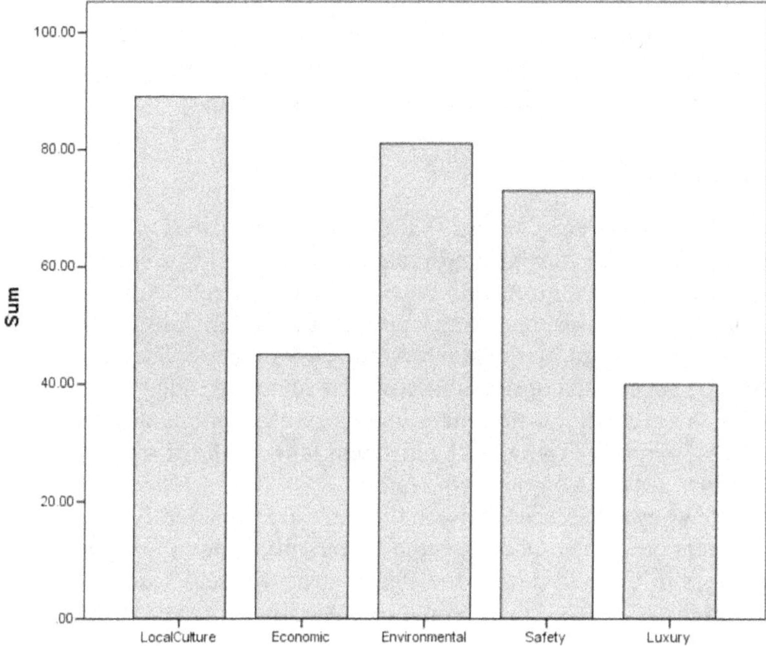

Figure 5.3 Frequencies of specific frames mentioned in tweets or retweeted links under the #CrystalSerenity.

The low occurrence of the economic frame represents the most significant contrast between traditional and social media; very little attention was devoted in social media to highlighting or assessing the potential economic benefits for Northern communities. A direct consequence of this was to underplay a frame widely perceived as positive, especially by Canadian users, even though some stops (like the one in Nome, Alaska) generated little economic benefits. The economic benefits of the Cambridge Bay stop were the main focus of interest, whereas little attention was paid to the other Canadian stops (in Ulukhaktok or Pond Inlet).

On the other hand, opinions on environmental issues were overwhelmingly negative, underlining the negative impacts on climate change and damages made to the pristine environment, especially the fauna, of the Arctic region.

Nonetheless, most of the media coverage focused on people rather than the environment. An environment-only perspective was criticized both by civil society (especially groups representing Inuit people, see Blake, August 17 2018) and scholars (see, e.g., Arnold, 2018), rendering Northerners invisible. The local culture and economic frames represent popular frames, combining for a more significant presence than coverage solely focusing on the Arctic environment.

Crisis averted

The Crystal Serenity cruise shared many similarities with the 1969 Manhattan transit: a ground-breaking, historical precedent, testing a new economic venture with vessels of unprecedented size for the region. In both cases, companies prepared for months to confront the safety risks posed by the harsh Arctic environment. The Manhattan transits generated considerable coverage on an extended time period, with the second transit generating substantial public attention; the Crystal Serenity experienced a different faith, with the second voyage barely registering on the media radar.

A few key differences between the two expeditions can explain these different outcomes. Of course, the sovereignty issue caused passionate uproars in Canada during the 1969 transit, whereas sovereignty was a non-factor for the cruise ship. Moreover, the reactive posture of the federal government and the lengthy legislative process ensured that the tanker's transit would remain at the top of the political agenda during the Winter and Spring of 1970. The nature of the 1969 trip also differed substantially from the Crystal Serenity trip. The environmental risk posed by the Manhattan was clearer and more straightforward for the Canadian public; the very nature of the tanker made it so that the risk of an oil spill was front and centre in the public imagery. On the other hand, the cruise ship did not pose such risk, but generated possible positive impacts (economically) for Northerners, something that the Manhattan could not do.

A quick glance at the nature of the media coverage (in Table 5.3, e.g.) can provide a convincing explanation as to why the Crystal Serenity transits did not translate into a national crisis in Canada and why attention subsided significantly (to the point of being a non-story in most media, social or traditional) by the second trip. Positive frames clearly outweighed negative ones in Canada, whereas the same trend could not be observed for non-Canadian users.

Precautions implemented by the cruise line clearly rebutted the majority of criticisms on three important fronts: respect of local culture/communities, economic benefits, and safety risks. The local culture and economic benefits angles provided positive coverage for

Table 5.3 Dominant perception of tweets on each frame during the two Crystal Serenity transits

	Tweets from Canadian users		*Tweets from non-Canadian users*		*Total*
	Dominantly positive	*Dominantly negative*	*Dominantly positive*	*Dominantly negative*	
Local culture frame	38	7	26	13	84
Environmental frame	5	17	1	42	65
Safety frame	9	12	17	14	52
Economic frame	20	1	14	6	41
Luxury frame	4	10	9	9	32
Total	76	47	67	84	274

the cruise ship, whereas the safety precautions undertaken ensured readers that safety risks were taken seriously. Only the environmental and luxury frames were left with negative perceptions, with the former being more prevalent. It is interesting to note that the precautionary measures related to safety and consultation/cooperation with local communities were acknowledged profusely, whereas concerns related to the environment were usually not presented to the audience.

In fact, an oft-repeated analytical observation was that Crystal Cruises had deep pockets and could, therefore, ensure that all precautions had been taken to guarantee a transit respectful of local communities, safety concerns, and (some) environmental damages to the Arctic ecosystem. However, the leading apprehension was that other operators might feel tempted to enter the Arctic cruise market; these companies might not cater to customers seeking luxury cruises and might not possess the means (or the will) to implement this precautionary outlook. According to Michael Byers,

> although the Crystal Serenity is well-managed and should have an uneventful trip, it will be followed by many other large ships, some from companies with dubious safety records. Not all of the risks associated with these ships can be addressed under the 46-year-old Arctic waters law.
>
> (Byers, August 12 2016: p. A11)

It represents an arduous endeavour to sensationalize the Crystal Serenity as a significant threat when the trips were described as "well-managed" and most observers expected an "uneventful trip." It is difficult in this context to dramatize or single out the cruise ship. The Crystal Serenity, after all, did not represent a direct threat; subsequent, low-budget cruises could potentially represent a more dangerous phenomenon.

Both traditional and social media offered a positive coverage of the events. Frames differed to a certain extent, with the economic story downplayed at the detriment of the safety angle in social media. The economic frame required somewhat more depth on the part of Twitter users as the focus had to be on testimonies of local Northerners about the economic benefits generated by the excursions. Other than retweeting external sources (especially from traditional media, which many did not, see Table 5.2), it was difficult for users to tackle this aspect on their own. The safety angle, on the other hand, was more conducive for observations or analysis; the risks and precautions taken by the company were obvious and highly conjectural.

The transits were again a clear illustration of media coverage on Arctic issues in the age of governance. A handful of articles and tweets evoked Canadian Arctic sovereignty but they represented exceptions rather than the norm. Environmental concerns, safety risks, and economic development necessarily lead to more complex and nuanced debates and assessments than black-or-white statements on possession and ownership, even in the echo chamber of social media.

Notes

1 In the case of the 2016 and 2017 voyages, this meant analysing the period spanning from 1 August to 30 September of each year.
2 The newspapers were: *Calgary Herald, Chronicle Herald, Edmonton Journal, Globe and Mail, La Presse, Le Devoir, Leader Post, Montreal Gazette, National Post, Ottawa Citizen, The Province,* and *Vancouver Sun.*
3 The Crystal Serenity can be credited for shining a light on the region, which had the indirect effect of raising awareness on the impact of melting ice and high food prices.
4 Of course, not all Twitter users include hashtags in all of their publications. However, Canadian users seem to make good use of this classification tool: about 70% of Canadian users incorporate hashtags in their publications on the platform.
5 Messages that included the hashtag but were off topic were discarded. For example, quite a few New Age enthusiasts praised the curative virtues of crystals using the #CrystalSerenity hashtag; these tweets were removed from the sample. Moreover, tweets which consisted only of photos or hashtags and exempt from text were also discarded from the analysis.
6 Many tweets were considered neutral as they could not be coded as either sharing positive or negative sentiments towards the cruise ship. Numerous tweets, for example, only briefed their network on the location of the Crystal Serenity at a given time.

7 National status was determined by browsing the Twitter handles of users. Users who did not share their location were included in the non-Canadian category.

References

Adi, Ana, Erickson, Kristofer and Lilleker, Darren. 2014. Elite Tweets: Analyzing the Twitter Communication Patterns of Labour Party Peers in the House of Lords. *Policy and Internet*, volume 6, issue 1: pp. 1–27.

Arnold, Elizabeth. 2018. Doom and Gloom: The Role of the Media in Public Disengagement on Climate Change. Shorenstein Center on Media, Politics and Public Policy. Harvard Kennedy School, available at https://shorensteincenter.org/wp-content/uploads/2018/05/Media-and-Climate-Change-Elizabeth-Arnold.pdf?x78124

Bajkiewicz, Timothy, Kraus, Jeffrey and Hong, Soo Yeon. 2011. The Impact of Newsroom Changes and the Rise of Social Media on the Practice of Media Relations. *Public Relations Review*, volume 37: pp. 329–31.

Blake, Emily. 2018. National Geographic Polar Bear Apology Proves Colonialist Attitudes Towards Inuit Remain, Say Northerners. *CBC News*, August 17 2018, available at www.rcinet.ca/eye-on-the-arctic/2018/08/17/inuit-nunavut-national-geographic-polar-bear-apology-indigenous-canada-colonialism-conservation-sealegacy/

Byers, Michael. August 12 2016. PM Should Move Now to Safeguard Northwest Passage. *Globe and Mail*, p. A11.

CBC Television. September 12 2016. Massive Cruise Ship Brings New Era of Arctic Tourism to Cambridge Bay. *The National*.

Comer, Bryan, Olmer, Naya and Mao, Xiaoli. 2016. Heavy Fuel Oil Use in Arctic Shipping in 2015. Working Paper 21, The International Council on Clean Transportation, available at www.theicct.org/sites/default/files/publications/HFO%20Arctic%20Shipping_working-paper_vF_21102016.pdf

Dawson, Jackie, Johnston, Margaret and Stewart, Emma. 2017. The Unintended Consequences of Regulatory Complexity: The Case of Cruise Tourism in Arctic Canada. *Marine Policy*, issue 76: pp. 71–8.

Dawson, Jackie, Stewart, Emma, Lemelin, Harvey and Scott, Daniel. 2010. The Carbon Cost of Polar Bear Viewing Tourism in Churchill, Canada. *Journal of Sustainable Tourism*, volume 18, issue 3: pp. 319–36.

DiStasio, Marcia and Bortree, Denise Sevick. 2012. Multi-method Analysis of Transparency in Social Media Practices: Survey, Interviews, and Content Analysis. *Public Relations Review*, volume 38: pp. 511–4.

Dubois, Elizabeth, and Gaffney, Devin. 2014. The Multiple Facets of Influence: Identifying Political Influentials and Opinion Leaders on Twitter. *American Behavioral Scientist*, volume 58, issue 10: pp. 1260–77.

Eijgelaar, Eke, Thaper, Carla and Peeters, Paul. 2010. Antarctic Cruise Tourism: The Paradoxes of Ambassadorship, "Last Chance Tourism" and

Greenhouse Gas Emissions. *Journal of Sustainable Tourism*, volume 18, issue 3: pp. 337–54.

Government of Nunavut. Responsible Cruise Tourism Development in Nunavut. Northern Public Affairs, October 2016, available at www.northernpublicaffairs.ca/index/responsible-cruise-tourism-development-in-nunavut/

Green, Geoff. 2010. Students on Ice: Learning in the Greatest Classrooms on Earth. In Michael Lück, Patrick T. Maher and Emma J. Stewart (eds.) Cruise Tourism in Polar Regions, Earthscan Publications, London: pp. 93–105.

Grimwood, Bryan. 2015. Advancing Tourism's Moral Morphology: Relational Metaphors for Just and Sustainable Arctic Tourism. *Tourist Studies*, volume 15, issue 1: pp. 3–26.

Grudz, Anatoliy and Roy, Jeffrey. 2014. Investigating Political Polarization on Twitter: A Canadian Perspective. *Policy and Internet*, volume 6, issue 1: pp. 28–45.

Himelboim, Itai, Hansen, Derek, and Bowser, Anna. 2013. Playing in the Same Twitter Network – Political Information Seeking in the 2010 US Gubernatorial Elections. *Information, Communication and Society*, volume 16, issue 9: pp. 1373–96.

Hopper, Tristan. August 30 2016. Ship Puts Nunavut Hamlet on the Map. *Ottawa Citizen*, p. 1.

Kajàn, Eva. 2013. An Integrated Methodological Framework: Engaging Local Communities in Arctic Tourism Development and Community-Based Adaptation. *Current Issues in Tourism*, volume 16, issue 3: pp. 286–301.

Klein, Ross. 2010. Cruises and Bruises: Safety, Security and Social Issues on Polar Cruises. In Michael Lück, Patrick T. Maher and Emma J. Stewart (eds.) Cruise Tourism in Polar Regions, Earthscan Publications, London: pp. 57–74.

Lachlan, Kenneth, Spence, Patric, Lin, Xialing, Najarian, Kristy and Del Greco, Maria. 2016. Social Media and Crisis Management: CERC, Search Strategies, and Twitter Content. *Computers in Human Behaviour*, volume 54: pp. 647–52.

Landriault, Mathieu. 2013. La sécurité arctique 2000–2010: une décennie turbulente? Ph.D. Dissertation, University of Ottawa, available at www.ruor.uottawa.ca/handle/10393/24353

Landriault, Mathieu. 2016. Interest and Public Perceptions on Canadian Arctic Sovereignty: Evidence from Editorials, 2000–2014. *International Journal of Canadian Studies*, volume 54: pp. 5–25.

Lasserre, Frédéci and Têtu, Pierre-Louis. 2015. The Cruise Tourism Industry in the Canadian Arctic: Analysis of Activities and Perceptions of Cruise Ship Operators. *Polar Record*, volume 51, issue 1: pp. 24–38.

Lemelin, Harvey, Dawson, Jackie, Stewart, Emma, Maher, Patrick and Lueck, Michael. 2010. Last-Chance Tourism: The Boom, Doom, and Gloom of Visiting Vanishing Destinations. *Current Issues in Tourism*, volume 13, issue 5: pp. 477–93.

Lück, Michael, Maher, Patrick and Stewart, Emma. 2010. *Cruise Tourism in Polar Regions – Promoting Environmental and Social Sustainability?* Earthscan Publications, London.

McWhinnie, Lauren, Halliday, William, Insley, Stephen, Hilliard, Casey and Canessa, Rosaline. 2018. Vessel Traffic in the Canadian Arctic: Management Solutions for Minimizing Impacts on Whales in a Changing Northern Region. *Ocean and Coastal Management*, issue 160; pp. 1–17.

Migdal, Alex. August 20 2016. Ship Sets a Clean Path through Arctic Channel. *Globe and Mail*, p. A6.

Murthy, Dhiraj. 2015. Twitter and Elections: Are Tweets Predictive, Reactive, or a Form of Buzz? *Information, Communication and Society*, volume 18, Issue 7: pp. 816–31.

Orams, Mark. 2010. Polar Yacht Cruising. In Michael Lück, Patrick T. Maher and Emma J. Stewart (eds.) *Cruise Tourism in Polar Regions*, Earthscan Publications, London: pp. 13–22.

Orlinsky, Katie and Holland, Eva. September 8 2016. Apocalypse Tourism? Cruising the Melting Arctic Ocean. Blommberg Businessweek, available at www.bloomberg.com/features/2016-crystal-serenity-northwest-passage-cruise/

Pincus, Rebecca. 2015. Large-Scale Disaster Response in the Arctic: Are We Ready? *Arctic Yearbook*, pp. 234–46.

Robbins, Mike. 2007. Development of Tourism in Arctic Canada. In John Snyder and Bernard Stonehouse (eds.) Prospects for Polar Tourism. CAB International Press, Wallingford: pp. 84–101.

Small, Tamara. 2011. What the Hashtag? A Content Analysis of Canadian Politics on Twitter. *Information, Communication and Society*, volume 14, issue 6: pp. 872–95.

Snyder, John and Stonehouse, Bernard (eds.). 2007. *Prospects for Polar Tourism*. CAB International Press, Wallingford.

Snyder, John. 2007a. Polar Tourism Markets. In John Snyder and Bernard Stonehouse (eds.) *Prospects for Polar Tourism*. CAB International Press, Wallingford: pp. 102–22, 51–70.

Snyder, John. 2007b. The Economic Role of Arctic Tourism. In John Snyder and Bernard Stonehouse (eds.) *Prospects for Polar Tourism*. CAB International Press, Wallingford: pp. 102–22.

Statista, June 15 2018. Number of Twitter Users in Canada from 2012 to 2021, available at www.statista.com/statistics/303875/number-of-twitter-users-canada/

Statistics Canada. 2016. Spotlight on Canadians: Results from the General Social Survey. Released on February 15 2016, available at www150.statcan.gc.ca/n1/pub/89-652-x/89-652-x2016001-eng.htm

Stewart, Emma and Dawson, Jackie. 2011. A Matter of Good Fortune? The Grounding of the *Clipper Adventurer* in the Northwest Passage, Arctic Canada. Arctic, volume 64, issue 2: pp. 263–7.

Stonehouse, Bernard and Snyder, John. 2010. *Polar Tourism – An Environmental Perspective*. Channel View Publications, Bristol.

Waters, Richard and Jamal, Jia. 2011. Tweet, Tweet, Tweet: A Content Analysis of Nonprofit Organizations' Twitter Updates. *Public Relations Review*, volume 37: pp. 321–4.

Weber, Bob. 2016. Northern Tourism – New Rules Considered for Arctic Cruises. *Chronicle-Herald*, Halifax, Nova Scotia: p. A6.

World Wildlife Fund. December 9 2016. Canada Should Modernize Grey Water Discharge Rules for the Arctic, WWF-Canada says, available at www.wwf.ca/?23481/Canada-should-modernize-grey-water-discharge-rules-for-the-Arctic-WWF-Canada-says

Zak, Annie. Northwest Passage Cruise from Alaska Won't Return Next Year. *Anchorage Daily News*, September 22 2017, available at www.adn.com/business-economy/2017/09/21/northwest-passage-cruise-from-alaska-wont-return-next-year/

Conclusion

The Arctic and the Canadian media

This book had for objective to empirically document how the Canadian media represented the Arctic region in the public sphere. The media has the potential to inform (or misinform) the Canadian populace and decision-makers about the challenges and opportunities the region faces. As such, it plays a crucial role as a socializing agent propagating specific interpretations of Arctic reality. The task of studying media representations is now more imperative than ever as we have observed great fragmentation in the media sector and democratization of information brought forth by social media platforms.

It is tempting, in this type of environment, to turn the spotlights on media reports that are grossly inaccurate or caricaturing reality. This selection bias should be avoided, however, in order to conduct a more rigorous analysis of long-term patterns in Arctic media coverage in Canada.

For the purpose of this book, 628 newspaper articles, 110 televised reports, 9 magazine articles, and 404 tweets were analysed to provide a thick empirical investigation of agenda setting, political messaging, and framing about the Arctic region in Canada.

Agenda setting

Agenda setting is typically an uncertain outcome for the media. Far-away regions, such as the Arctic, are generally deemed more susceptible to agenda setting as most people could not experience them in their daily lives: hence, the media could mediate and familiarize the public to these distant events. Did this materialize for Arctic issues?

The nature of the issue alone cannot explain why agenda setting does or does not work. Agenda setting was more manifest during the 1985 Polar Sea incident. However, mass media could not generate interest and manufacture news on their own; the activism and initiatives of other key societal actors were pivotal to shine the national spotlights on the transit. Academics, civil society and Inuit groups were all active players, reacting to the event and calling on the government to act.

A similar dynamic was at play during the 1969–1970 Manhattan transits. Opposition parties, especially the Conservatives, questioned incessantly the Liberal government about its management of the tanker's transits.

The 2016 voyage of the Crystal Serenity did register significant media coverage, although attention dissipated quickly. As we observed when analysing social media coverage, proponents and opponents (including many non-governmental organizations) voiced their opinions, with positive perceptions outweighing negative ones. The support of local communities, in contrast with the 1985 Polar Sea crisis, constitutes another mitigating factor.

The incorporation of the event in broader narratives represents another key factor explaining the occurrence of agenda setting. The 1969 Manhattan and 1985 Polar Sea crises were about much more than the Arctic; the continental energy policy (for the first crisis) and the Canada-US relationship (for both) loomed large in media reports. The conciliatory approach of Prime Minister Brian Mulroney towards the American neighbour in 1985 was cited in numerous journalistic articles as the main reason why the US disregarded Canadian sovereignty claims. The reflection then centred on evaluating whether the Polar Sea transit was reason enough to discard the rapprochement with the US partner.

It should be mentioned that these broader narratives on their own are not sufficient to generate the necessary amount of attention. The 2000–2005 period is a case in point: media coverage remained limited during that time period even as global warming and a melting Arctic were starting to form emerging phenomenon. Controversial and novel developments along with incidents ripe with powerful symbols and actors must happen for media coverage to follow.

Furthermore, sovereignty issues have the potential to set the agenda as we have seen in Chapter 1. The day-to-day management of practical questions and the dynamics of governance, with its coordination among numerous stakeholders, are less conducive to agenda setting. These circumpolar relations typically do not culminate in showdowns or confrontation but rather in realistic and pragmatic cooperation to achieve a common goal. The 2010–2015 period, covered in Chapter 4, offers the best illustration of this effect: the necessities of economic development in a (still) difficult environment makes cooperation with sovereign states a necessity. It would appear that it is more difficult to make headlines with pragmatic cooperation rather than confrontation or public disagreements…

Based on the evidence gathered, crises brought forward by the media are unlikely to happen in the near future, unless we are faced with a clear and serious challenge to Canadian Arctic sovereignty. In fact, more positive coverage of Arctic issues during the 2010–2015 period coincided with more support for seeking compromises and negotiations in Canadian public opinion.

Political messaging

Agenda setting means that the media may impose stories or items figuring at the top of the political agenda. Political messaging, for its part, translates in the opposite: the political elite, governments, and elected representatives would dictate their messages and control the political agenda by utilizing the media. The evidence gathered in this book informs us that political messaging of governments can vary greatly in nature.

For example, the management of the 1969 crisis by the Trudeau government may be categorized as counterproductive. A shifting position, with contradictory public declarations from key members of Cabinet, contributed to sustained media coverage of the issue. The calendar did not help as the second transit was announced as the new policy on Arctic environmental protection was being developed. Policymaking on the fly is typically not conducive to coherent political messaging, and it would seem that the Manhattan transits were no exception to the rule. Opaque or vague answers from ministers called for more scrutiny from opposition parties, who were determined to score political points on this issue.

As a result, the Manhattan crisis was prolonged before subsiding, with media attention continuing right until the legislation was presented to the House of Commons.

On the other side of the spectrum, governmental initiatives can help to control political communication diffused in the media. For example, the annual summer Arctic tours, initiated by Prime Minister Stephen Harper, allowed government to showcase the PM. It also offered a great platform to efficiently promote adopted investments and measures through daily press conferences and announcements. Some criticisms were expressed by reporters but these critical voices represented a minority and did not fundamentally undermine the government's Arctic policy.

A similar effect was observed with the reestablishment of Arctic exercises by the Canadian military through the NARWHAL and NANOOK operations. From 2000 to 2005, the bulk of media coverage on the Arctic in Canada peaked immediately before, during, or after these military exercises. Many Canadian Forces personnel were interviewed in major dailies and this emphasis highlighted increased activism by the Canadian government with the intent to adapt to a changing Arctic.

Of course, political messaging cannot always succeed in reaching its objective; the media did not always react to cues initiated by government. Reorientation of political communication proved to be laborious and ineffective at times: the Harper government's Arctic messaging from 2010 to 2015 suffered this fate. As covered in Chapter 3, the conservative government transitioned from a focus on sovereignty (roughly from 2006 to 2009) to a more pragmatic policy showcasing announcements and investments on human capital (after 2010). The Prime ministerial annual tours reflected this evolution, shying away from the use-it-or-lose-it rhetoric.

In this context, it is not surprising that the northern protectionist outburst by the Harper government in early 2014 did not fundamentally change the state of media discourse on the region. Hence, the global interconnectedness frame continued to prevail in the Canadian media, with a focus on governance rather than sovereignty issues.

Framing

Based on anecdotal evidence, one would have expected to find frames related to common tropes of Arctic competition/confrontation and race at the detriment of ones documenting cooperation and order. The evidence gathered in this book offers a more nuanced appraisal of media coverage. Without a doubt, the competition/race frame is a popular narrative, one that journalists without specific knowledge of the region relied on: the coverage of the Prime ministerial summer tours illustrated this tendency. The picture is different when longer time periods are analysed.

Indeed, if the competition and race frames were prevalent during the 2000–2005 period, a frame projecting positive interconnectedness proved to be dominant from 2010 to 2015. Anticipations and predictions from 2000 to 2005 projected a darker regional context. However, reality later set in and was subsequently reflected in media representations; it should be a humble lesson that predictions are a highly speculative game.

Likewise, frames can be articulated in novel ways. The confrontation and race frames were often fused into one, describing the Arctic as under intense competitive dynamics. The fusion of these frames evolved during the 2010–2015 period. Some articles described the region as one subjected to high demands yet free of conflict while other journalistic reports highlighted disputes while stressing the significant barriers preventing an "Arctic rush".

Moreover, the audience could be presented with multiple issue frames for the same story as the media coverage of the Crystal Serenity demonstrated. Economic, safety, environmental, and local culture frames intertwined, often in the same article or tweet, informing readers about different aspects of the voyages. Again, positive perceptions, akin to the global interconnectedness frame covered in Chapter 4, were widespread emphasizing the possible economic benefits and the respect of local communities displayed by the cruise line. In this case, traditional and social media helped society understand the complexity of the matter at hand, refraining from using the most obvious frame (environmental) at the detriment of all others.

Furthermore, this book documented how framing can originate from many different sources. Journalists framed the Arctic by describing the region in certain ways and focusing on specific angles, while reporters typically relied on darker assessments of Arctic geopolitics, as presented in Chapters 2 and 3. By performing such evaluations, they implicitly took position by promoting one interpretation about the state of the region. At other times, they voiced criticisms about governmental initiatives, as was evidenced in the media coverage during the annual Prime ministerial tours.

Experts were sought after to offer their viewpoints and shed light on recent developments. These external actors represent an under-studied group. As Chapters 2 and 3 demonstrated, these experts deserve more scholarly attention as they constitute a precious resource for journalists, as they helped reporters weave a thick narrative about their subject matter and provided authoritative analysis on Arctic politics. The nature of the opinions expressed by these external actors should not be considered a given: Canadian Forces personnel can diffuse optimistic or pessimistic perceptions of Arctic geopolitics.

A fascinating time: Media analysis in the age of Arctic governance

This study represents one of the first attempts at empirically documenting media coverage on Arctic issues in Canada. As such, it constitutes a departing point, leaving some questions unanswered and thus opening numerous potential avenues for future research.

New media

The bulk of this book focused its attention on traditional media: the rise of new media in people's information consumption habits must be seriously accounted for in academic work. This evidently represents a daunting task for any media analyst; the sheer mass of information available to the population has multiplied exponentially with specialized publications, blogs, and social media. In any given day, hundreds of tweets are published with the hashtag #Arctic, in English alone. As far as political messaging is concerned, 551 tweets written by Canadian elected representatives mentioned the term "Arctic" in 2017. This, in turn, renders a rigorous analysis of media coverage more difficult: information that is more fragmented and traditional as well as novel sources compete to offer appealing content to their readership or viewership. We will need new methods and analytical tools to make sense of this massive amount of media communication.

Influence

Of course, the media is typically not analysed in isolation. This book attempted to assess the effects of media representation on governmental decision-making and public opinion. This could prove to be challenging as very few surveys are conducted interrogating people on their attitudes towards Arctic issues. The only large-scale survey available for study (the Rethinking the Top of the World polls sponsored by the Munk-Gordon Arctic Security programme) covered multiple Arctic countries. However, it was only performed every five years: causality is difficult to assess over such a long period of time.[1]

The rise of new media could help on this front. Indeed, the emergence of social media has also served to blur the line between news providers and the audience; social media users can also be active participants in debates and conversations. This phenomenon offers a great opportunity to better assess the potential of social media for influence and persuasion; the popularity of different messages can be evaluated by studying the frequency at which specific news pieces are relayed by users. Focusing on why and how specific stories become viral can provide insights into networks of influence on social media.

This could partially fulfil a shortcoming we are currently experiencing with public opinion; polls on Arctic issues in Canada are rare, rendering any analytical connection between public opinion and the media perilous.

At the same time, analysing the content published on social media can inform us on the types of messages diffused by key influencing actors. It does not, on the other hand, sheds light on how the audience receive and interpret specific messages that they are exposed to. There is much work to be undertaken on this facet in order to uncover how information (old or new) is processed by individuals and whether or not this information changes perceptions on Arctic issues. The use of experiments and focus groups could improve our understanding of how people react to information.

The Canadian media in comparative perspective

The Canadian media were at the centre of academic investigation in this book. Of course, in a globalized media landscape, the media in Canada constitutes only one piece of the puzzle. With generalized access to the internet, Canadians and global citizens now have access to local and international publications at their fingertips.

Looking back at the Crystal Serenity voyages, articles written by international and local media were also among the most forwarded by social media users. *Slate*, National Geographic, Al Jazeera and the *Washington Post* were among these media, forming an heterogeneous group to say the least.[2] There is a tendency in these publications to frame Arctic development in broader narratives, be it climate change, the rise of China or Russia's re-emergence. On the other hand, local media, such as the Nunatsiaq News or the KNOM radio mission, can bring novel frames to the fore, providing counter-narratives to national and international news outlets. Local media can offer valuable insights into people's experiences and the impacts of global phenomenon on local communities. For example, they embodied a great source of local information during the 2016 Crystal Serenity voyage.

The Canadian media coverage must also be compared with coverage originating from other countries, especially Arctic ones. So far, academic work has mostly focused on documenting coverage in one Arctic state. A collaborative endeavour is necessary to map the representations prevalent in different Arctic countries. In fact, the multiplicity of languages in the region calls for such a cooperative project. This would complete the picture, allowing comparative insights between the Canadian media, the media in other Arctic states, and the global media.

Crises and eras

Finally, attention must be given to both studying media coverage of specific crises or incidents and in longer time periods. Crises monopolize public awareness and have a lasting effect on public consciousness. As such, they are intense periods creating powerful symbols. The impact of the 1969 Manhattan and the 1985 Polar Sea crises was felt years after the actual event. However, these developments usually occur in a compressed timespan and constitute the exception rather than the norm. They typically generate significant scholarly interest in media analysis since the number of sources is limited and comparison between different media sources is feasible.

Nonetheless, greater attention should be paid to the evaluation of extended time periods. Such focus could provide a more accurate understanding of the broader media landscape, allowing one to detect changes and evolution in media coverage. By the same token, media attention during crises could be understood in a broader context as either exacerbating or mitigating these outbursts.

This monograph was of an exploratory nature as I covered the beginning of the climate change era (2000–2005) and its acceleration (2010–2015); human activity will only increase as the global melt worsens. Media representations of the Arctic region will undoubtedly multiply as new actors utilize the region and its waterways for economic development and cultural exchanges. The relevance of studying media coverage of the region has never been greater; it is imperative that we seize this opportunity to analyse media coverage in a rigorous, objective and empirically grounded manner.

Notes

1 The Munk-Gordon Arctic Security programme was discontinued, meaning the end of the Rethinking the Top of the world polls. No poll is scheduled in the near future.

2 The *Slate* magazine article was the most retweeted publications in our sample, surpassing more reputable publications such as the *New York Times* or the *Washington Post*.

Index

Note: **Bold** page numbers refer to tables.

www.ingramcontent.com/pod-product-compliance
Lightning Source LLC
LaVergne TN
LVHW010925110826
845149LV00013B/2481

* 9 7 8 1 0 3 2 2 4 0 2 1 3 *